Keynote for iPad

TOM NEGRINO

 Peachpit Press

Visual QuickStart Guide
Keynote for iPad
Tom Negrino

Peachpit Press
1249 Eighth Street
Berkeley, CA 94710
510/524-2178
510/524-2221 (fax)

Find us on the Web at www.peachpit.com
To report errors, please send a note to errata@peachpit.com

Peachpit Press is a division of Pearson Education

Project Editor: Nancy Peterson
Developmental, Copy, and Technical Editor: Dori Smith
Production Editor: Myrna Vladic
Compositor: Jerry Ballew
Indexer: Karin Arrigoni
Cover Design: The Visual Group
Interior Design: Peachpit Press

ISBN-13: 978-0-321-75139-3
ISBN-10:   0-321-75139-6

9 8 7 6 5 4 3 2 1

Printed and bound in the United States of America

Dedication

I'd like to dedicate this, my 40th book, to all of the editors I've worked with through the years. Thanks for teaching me to be a better writer.

My personal Editorial Hall of Fame includes:

Cheryl England

Carol Person

Marjorie Baer

Linda Wooldridge

Scholle McFarland

And always, Nancy Davis.

Special Thanks to:

My patient and exacting editor, Dori Smith, who made my work better and encouraged me when a very challenging schedule seemed overwhelming.

Thanks to Peachpit's Nancy Peterson for instigating and shepherding this project to completion, and for her fine editorial sensibilities.

Thanks to Myrna Vladic, for her excellent production work.

Thanks to the book's compositor, Jerry Ballew, and thanks to Karin Arrigoni for the index.

Thanks to Peachpit's Nancy Ruenzel for her support.

Thanks to my friend Jeff Carlson for his indispensable reference, *The iPad Pocket Guide*.

I thank, acknowledge, and credit the following Flickr users for their fine photographs, used under a Creative Commons license:

Boltron http://flic.kr/p/72i98o

Dave Photography http://flic.kr/p/7pkjTN

Star5112 http://flic.kr/p/NVGZK and http://flic.kr/p/NV4nb

Jinxmcc http://flic.kr/p/8mpA98

TheNickster http://flic.kr/p/29t2Dg

In my office, the soundtrack for this book included music from my Pandora and Rhapsody subscriptions, and lots more bouncy pop music.

Contents at a Glance

Table of Contents

Introduction

Welcome to *Keynote for iPad: Visual QuickStart Guide*. As the author of the first book about Keynote for Macintosh, I'm excited to also have the opportunity to write a book about the mobile version, Keynote for iPad.

I start the book with an overview of Keynote, move on to creating your first presentation, and then discuss how to add content and interactivity. Finally, I show you how to give the presentation effectively.

You'll be able to use what you learn to build your own presentations, such as a talk for your annual sales meeting, a lecture for a class, or a slide show for your department detailing your latest work.

Using this book

I've organized the different elements of building presentations with Keynote for iPad (henceforth, just "Keynote"; when I discuss Keynote for Mac, I'll refer to "Keynote '09") into chapters, and within each chapter are numbered, step-by-step directions that tell you exactly how to accomplish various tasks. You don't have to work through the entire book in order, but it is structured so the more complex material builds on the earlier tasks.

TIP Throughout the book I've included many tips that will help you get things done faster, better, or both.

TIP Be sure to read the figure captions, too; sometimes you'll find extra nuggets of information there.

TIP When I'm showing Web and email addresses, I've used this code font.

TIP You'll also find sidebars (with colored backgrounds) that delve deeper into subjects.

Working with the iPad

The iPad's multi-touch interface brings a whole new set of terminology, and you'll find it easier to use this book once you understand the terms I'm using. Here are the terms I use in the book, with explanations of what they mean.

- **Tapping** means to point at an area on the screen and then lightly tap it with one finger. Similarly, **double-tapping** simply means to tap the same object on the screen twice in rapid succession.

- A **popover** is iPad's equivalent of a dialog in Mac or Windows. It's a list of options that appears when you tap a button. For example, in Keynote, tapping the Media button on the toolbar brings up this popover **A** (the Charts button in the popover has also been tapped).

  Tapping one of the chart types in the popover inserts a chart of that type onto your slide.

- **Slow double-tapping** is a term I invented for this book. It means that you tap an object, pause briefly, and then tap it again. In Keynote, this is often how you select objects and bring up popovers that allow you to edit them **B**.

- When you **touch and hold**, you'll place your finger on an object on the screen, maintaining contact.

- To **drag**, touch and hold a point on the screen and then move your finger across. You can drag objects around on a Keynote slide, or you can drag inside a popover to scroll through a list of options.

- A **flick** is like a drag, but you do it more quickly. It's usually used to scroll things faster. The iPad's software notes the velocity of your finger and then matches the motion, until the scrolling object gradually slows and comes to a stop.

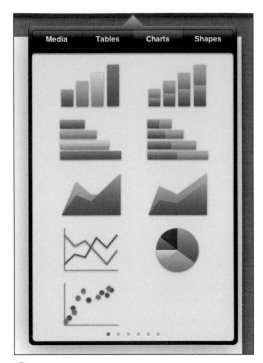

A The Charts pane of the Media popover.

B A slow double-tap brings up this popover.

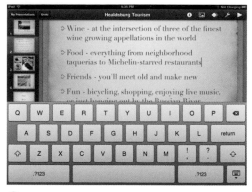

C The standard iPad onscreen keyboard.

D The onscreen keyboard includes the Shift and Symbol keys (top) and the Number key (bottom).

E Notice that this layout also includes an Undo key.

F This layout includes a Redo key.

- A **swipe** is a movement in between a drag and a flick, and usually horizontal. In A, for example, you can swipe right or left in the Charts popover to see different preset color choices for the charts. Notice the indicator at the bottom showing that there are six screens you can swipe through.

- A **pinch** gesture uses two fingers. You can zoom in or out on an item by touching two fingers to the screen and pinching them together (to zoom out) or spread them apart (to zoom in).

- Touch two fingers to the screen and turn your hand to **rotate** an object on a slide, such as a photo.

TIP You can often use two hands to accomplish tasks in Keynote. For example, if you want to select more than one slide at a time, it's easier to do it using both hands.

Using the iPad's Onscreen Keyboard

When you double-tap inside a text box in Keynote, the iPad's software keyboard slides up from the bottom of the screen C. You can type on this keyboard as you would a hardware keyboard, with a few caveats:

- Some characters don't appear where you expect them to, because the screen isn't big enough to accommodate a standard keyboard layout. For example, you type an exclamation point by holding the Shift key D and tapping the comma key.

- To get numbers and some frequently-used symbols, tap the Number key D, which changes the keyboard layout E.

- You can access lesser-used characters by first tapping the Number key and then tapping the Symbol key D, which displays yet another keyboard F.

continues on next page

- You can add a period by simply tapping two spaces after a word.
- To hide the keyboard, tap the Keyboard key .
- Caps Lock is disabled by default, but you can change that by going to Settings > General > Keyboard and turning on Enable Caps Lock. To activate Caps Lock when you are typing, double-tap the Shift key. The face of the key turns blue **G** to show that you are in Caps Lock mode.

TIP The easiest way to quickly insert a number or symbol on the screen shown in **E** is to touch and hold the Number key, slide your finger to the character you desire, and then lift your finger.

Selecting Text or Objects

In Keynote, you generally tap an object on your slide to select it. That object could be a text box **H**, a photo, a table, a chart, or a graphic object like a line or other geometric shape. A selected object on your slide will show selection handles.

Double-tapping a word inside a text box selects the word, highlighting it and causing selection handles to appear at the left and right edges of the word **I**.

You can drag either selection handle to expand or contract the selection. You can also tap one of the options in the Edit popover shown in **I** to cut, copy, or paste.

There's more online

To help you get up and running faster with Keynote, I've prepared some sample files with some of the content in this book that you can import and use for practice. You'll find those files on the Peachpit Web site, at **www.peachpit.com/vqs/KeynoteforiPad/**.

Let's get started

Every journey begins with a first step, and if you've read this far, your journey with Keynote has already begun. Thanks for joining me, don't forget to have fun, and let's get started building some presentations.

— Tom Negrino, September 2010

G The Keyboard key and the Shift key (shown with Caps Lock activated).

> Canoe leisurely down the Russian River

> Bicycle the best rides in Northern California

> Hike breathtaking nature trails

> Pick up a snack at the Farmer's Market

H A selected text box.

I A selected word.

Keynote for iPad Overview

Welcome to Keynote for iPad! Keynote, one of the mobile versions of the iWork productivity suite from Apple, is an exciting program that can help you create compelling presentations with a minimum of effort. Keynote's gorgeous themes, superior text handling, attractive animations, and excellent graphics capabilities allow you to deliver your ideas with maximum visual impact.

This visual punch doesn't come at the price of complexity; it's easy to build a Keynote presentation, whether you're a novice speaker or a polished presenter. But don't be fooled into thinking that because Keynote for iPad is easy to use and running on a mobile device, it lacks power; there's a lot of substance behind that pretty face.

In this chapter, you'll learn how to install and start Keynote, see an overview of the program's workspace, learn the parts of a Keynote slide, and ask the program for help. Let's get started with Keynote.

In This Chapter

Installing and Starting the App

Installing Keynote is as simple as installing any other app on your iPad. After just a few clicks of the mouse or taps on your iPad's screen, you'll be done.

To purchase and install Keynote via iTunes:

1. In iTunes, click the iTunes Store icon in the sidebar.

   The iTunes store appears.

2. In the Search Store field at the upper-right corner of the window, type "Keynote" and press Return.

3. If needed, scroll the screen until you see Keynote listed under iPad Apps.

4. Click Keynote. The app's description appears **Ⓐ**.

5. Click the Buy App button.

   The iTunes Store asks you to sign in (if you haven't already done so) and then downloads the Keynote app.

6. Connect your iPad to your computer.

   The iPad appears in the Devices section of the iTunes sidebar.

7. Click to select your iPad in the Devices section of the iTunes sidebar and then click the Sync button at the lower-right corner of the iTunes window.

   After the sync is complete, Keynote appears on one of your iPad's Home screens **Ⓑ**.

Ⓐ Click the Buy App button to purchase Keynote and download it to iTunes on your computer.

B After you install Keynote, it appears on one of your iPad's Home screens (in this case it's in the bottom row of applications, just above the applications in the iPad's Dock).

C To get a quick feel for Keynote, tap the Get Started presentation and then look through its slides.

To purchase and install Keynote from the App Store on the iPad:

1. Tap the App Store icon on your iPad.

2. In the Search field at the upper-right corner of the window, type "Keynote" and press Return.

   Keynote will appear as one of the found items.

3. Tap Keynote. The app's description appears.

4. Tap the button showing the app's price.

   The button changes to say Buy App.

5. Tap the Buy App button.

   The App Store will ask you to sign in with your password (if you haven't already done so) and then downloads Keynote, which then appears on one of your iPad's Home screens **B**.

To start Keynote:

Tap the Keynote icon on your iPad's screen.

The app opens **C**. There is a Get Started presentation already loaded that tells you a little about how to use Keynote.

Exploring the Keynote Workspace

The Keynote workspace is made up of one window with a number of sections **A**. Let's look at the pieces one by one.

The Slide Canvas

This is the main Keynote document window; it's where you'll edit your slide text and place graphics, tables, and charts.

The Slide Navigator

The Slide Navigator is the pane at the left edge of the document window. It shows thumbnails of your slides. The background of the selected slide in the Slide Navigator is highlighted. At the bottom of the Slide Navigator is the Add Slide button, which will be covered in Chapter 3.

Slide Navigator

Toolbar

Add Slide button

Slide Canvas

A The Keynote user interface is made up of three main areas : Slide Navigator, Slide Canvas, and Toolbar.

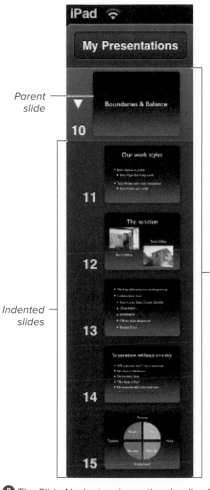

Parent slide

Indented slides

Slide group

B The Slide Navigator shows thumbnails of the slides in your presentation, with the currently selected slide highlighted. The Slide Navigator also allows you to group slides together, with the slides in a group, appearing indented in the list.

You can organize and group slides in this view by dragging slide thumbnails to the right so they are indented in the list, as shown in **B**. The parent slide of a group of indented slides has a disclosure triangle; tapping the triangle allows you to hide or show the indented slides. This makes it easier to organize the presentation, especially with longer shows. You can also drag the parent slide to another place in the presentation, and the indented slides move along with it.

Another thing you can do in the Slide Navigator is skip slides; skipped slides won't appear when you give the presentation, and will "collapse" in the Slide Navigator, appearing as a line. You'll learn more about grouping and skipping slides in Chapter 3.

The Toolbar

Like most programs, Keynote has a toolbar, which provides the tools you need to open, create, edit, and play presentations **C**. It has the following items:

- The **My Presentations** button leaves the main Keynote workspace and opens the My Presentations view, which shows you all the presentations you have in Keynote **D** (see the following page). You also use this view to create, rename, delete, and export presentations. More about this view in Chapter 2.

continues on next page

Transitions and Animations

Media

Info

Tools

Play

C Use the controls in Keynote's Toolbar to make changes to the current presentation.

- Tap the **Undo** button to undo the last action. You can tap it multiple times to undo your changes in sequence.

- The **Title** of your presentation appears in the middle of the toolbar.

- The **Info** button allows you to modify an item that you have selected on the Slide Canvas. When you tap the button, a *popover* appears (on the iPad, a popover serves the same purpose as a dialog in a Mac or Windows program). The popover displays appropriate choices, depending on the selected item; if you select a text box, the popover will be different than if you select a graphic **E**.

- The **Media** button produces a popover that gives you access to your Photo Libraries that you have synced to your iPad from iTunes, and also allows you to insert tables, charts, and graphic shapes on your slides.

- When you tap the **Transitions and Animations** button, Keynote shifts into a mode that allows you to add transitions between slides, or animate slide objects (such as text, graphic, table, and chart items). You'll learn more about using slide transitions and animations in Chapter 8.

- The **Tools** button gives you access to a variety of miscellaneous features, including finding and replacing text, turning on slide numbers, and the like. I'll be covering the items in the Tools popover throughout the book.

- Finally, the **Play** button plays your presentation full-screen on your iPad. If you have a Dock to video adapter cable, the presentation will also play on an external screen or a video projector.

D Swiping right or left in the My Presentations view allows you to switch between different presentations.

E The popover you get when you tap the Info button in the toolbar changes, depending on what you have selected in the Slide Canvas. Selected text gives you a very different popover (left) than a selected graphic (right).

Title placeholder   Background

Body Text placeholder   Image placeholder

A In addition to this slide's background image, there are three placeholders on this slide: two for text and one for an image.

B When you tap the Image button inside an Image placeholder, the Photo Albums popover appears, allowing you to select an image on your iPad.

Anatomy of a Slide

To make it easier to create your slides, Keynote provides *placeholders* on its slides, into which you can put text or graphics. These placeholders are arranged into preset *slide layouts*, and every slide in your presentation is based on one of these layouts. In Keynote for iPad, there are eight kinds of slide layouts from which to choose; more detail on the layout types coming up in Chapter 3. Besides the slide layout, each presentation also has a single *theme*, which provides its visual look, including things like the slide's background image and the style and color of the text you put on the slides.

Figure **A** shows a newly-created slide against the Slide Canvas. To make things easier to see, I've selected all three of the placeholders on the slide. Placeholders are part of the design of the theme, and you can think of them as slots for text, graphics, or movies that show you where the object will be added. Let's go into detail on each of the three placeholders on this slide and the slide background.

- The **Title** text placeholder is included on five of the eight available slide layouts (the Blank, Bullets, and Photo layouts don't need a title). The title is the main heading for each slide.

- A slide's **Body Text** is contained in one or more text boxes. The body text can be bulleted or numbered lists, a caption for an image, or plain text.

- An **Image** placeholder is a frame into which you can place an image or movie from the Photo Albums you previously synced to your iPad **B**.

- The **Background** is an image that is part of the theme.

Changing the Canvas Magnification

You can zoom into (or out of) the action by using the Pinch gesture. This is the gesture where you touch two fingers to the screen and pinch them together (to zoom out) or spread them apart (to zoom in). The four available magnifications are 50% 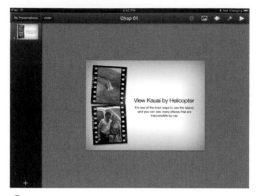; Fit, the normal view, which fills up most of the Slide Canvas and leaves only a little of the canvas visible in the background; Full Screen, which makes the Keynote interface go away and lets the slide take up the entire iPad screen (this is especially useful as a quick preview of how the slide will look during your presentation); and 200%, which lets you zoom in on a slide's details.

A To get a bird's eye view of your slide, zoom out to the 50% view.

To zoom in on a slide:

In the Slide Canvas, touch two fingers to the screen and spread them apart. If you want a higher magnification level, repeat the gesture.

To zoom out on a slide:

In the Slide Canvas, touch two fingers to the screen and pinch them together. If you want a lower magnification level, repeat the gesture.

TIP When you touch your fingers to the screen, make sure that you don't tap and select one of the items in the slide. It's easy to accidentally select and move a slide item. If you do, just tap the Undo button to put the misplaced item back where it belongs.

Getting On-Screen Help

Keynote comes with its own Help files, which are read in Safari. When you access Help, Safari launches and shows you the Help file. If you have an active connection on your iPad, Safari loads up-to-date versions from Apple's Web site. If you don't have Internet connectivity, Keynote uses the version of the Help files stored within the program.

To access the Help files:

1. Tap the Tools button in the toolbar.

   The Tools popover appears Ⓐ.

2. Tap the Go to Help item.

   Safari loads and displays the Help files Ⓑ.

Ⓑ On the iPad, Safari launches, showing you the help file.

TIP The Help files cover all three of the iWork programs: Keynote, Pages, and Numbers. So if you have more than one program, you can check information about any of them before you leave Safari and return to your iWork.

TIP Because the Help files are on the Web, if you have another computer handy, you can work on your iPad and still consult the Help files without leaving the particular iWork program you're using. Just use this URL in your computer's browser: `http://help.apple.com/iwork/safari/interface/`. The files may not look quite the same as on the iPad depending on what browser you're using 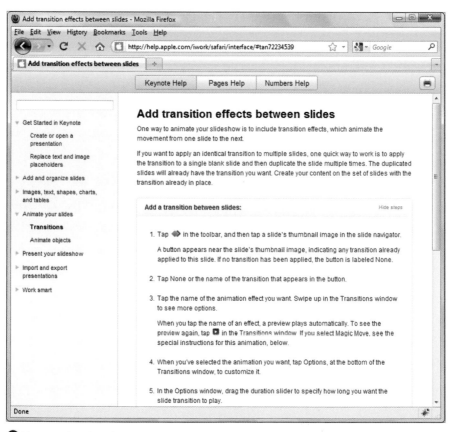.

TIP You can use Internet Explorer on Windows to view the help files, but they look best in Safari or Firefox for Windows.

C You can also view the help file in any Web browser on a computer. In this case, it looks a bit different because I'm using Firefox for Windows.

Bringing Documents into Keynote

While you can create complete presentations using Keynote for iPad, you're likely to want to import existing presentations that you created in Keynote '09, or with Microsoft PowerPoint for either Mac or Windows.

Using documents created in the desktop versions of the presentation programs in Keynote for iPad is a three-step process. In this chapter, you'll learn how to add compatible documents to iTunes, synchronize them to your iPad, and then finally import them into Keynote. I'll also discuss some of the limitations of the iPad version's importing process.

In This Chapter

Moving Documents to the iPad

File management on the iPad is, to be charitable, clunky. The iPad doesn't show up on your computer's desktop like any other USB device, and you can't get to any files or folders on the iPad directly. Instead, Apple has added a new section called File Sharing to the Apps tab of the increasingly-misnamed iTunes for Mac or Windows. In this section, each app on your iPad that supports File Sharing appears in a list. Clicking on the app in the list on the left shows you documents for that app in the list on the right . You can add files to the list, and they will be transferred to your iPad.

You can also bring documents to the iPad via the iPad's Mail app by receiving an email with a presentation file as an attachment. You can then open and import the attached file.

A third method to get files onto your iPad uses Apple's iWork.com, an online service that helps you share your iWork documents with you or others. You'll need to set up an account on iWork.com before you can work with it from your Mac and iPad.

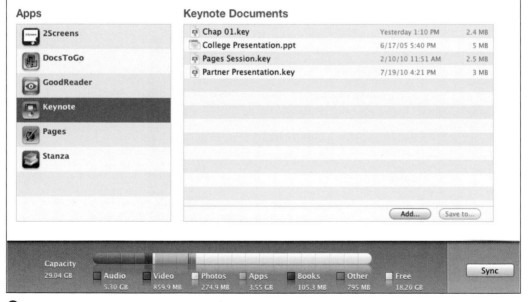

 You'll transfer presentation files to the iPad using the File Sharing section in iTunes.

▼ DEVICES
   ▼ 🖥 Tom Negrino's iPad ▭ ⏏
       🎵 Music
       🎬 Movies
       📺 TV Shows
       🎙 Podcasts   68
       📖 Books
       🖼 New Stuff
       🖼 Spoken Word
       🎵 Purchased

🅑 Select your iPad in iTunes's Devices section.

To add documents to File Sharing in iTunes:

1. Connect your iPad to your computer with a Dock Connector to USB cable.

   Your iPad will appear in iTunes's sidebar, under Devices 🅑.

2. Go to the Apps tab for your iPad. Scroll down to the File Sharing section at the bottom of the window 🅐.

3. In the left column of the File Sharing section, click Keynote.

4. Drag a file that you want to add from the Macintosh Finder or Windows Explorer into the Documents list.

   or

   At the bottom of the right column, click the Add button. iTunes displays a Choose a File dialog. Navigate to the file you want to add, select it, and click the Choose button.

   After a brief wait, iTunes copies the files in the Documents list to your iPad. You don't have to click the Sync button in iTunes for this to happen, and when File Sharing copies files, it doesn't perform a complete synchronization. Now you're ready to import the presentation into Keynote, as detailed in the next section.

TIP Unfortunately, there's no obvious way to tell the version of a Keynote file on your Mac. If you created a presentation in earlier versions of Keynote, I recommend that you first open the presentation in Keynote '09 or later, then choose File > Save As and save a copy of the document. Keynote will automatically save the document in the latest format, which will be compatible with Keynote for iPad. Then use the newly saved copy for File Sharing to the iPad.

TIP You can't synchronize your iPad to iTunes wirelessly; you must use a USB cable.

TIP You can also move files from the iPad to your computer using File Sharing; I'll cover how to do that in Chapter 10.

TIP If you like, you can add multiple documents to the Documents list at once, allowing you to transfer them all in one step.

TIP It's possible to add any kind of file to iTunes's File Sharing Documents list, but only files compatible with Keynote on the iPad will appear in Keynote's Import Presentation window, with one exception: a Keynote file created with any version of the program on the Mac will appear in the Import Presentation window. However, unless it is a Keynote '09 file, it won't import successfully.

To delete documents from the File Sharing list:

1. In the File Sharing section of the Apps tab of iTunes **A**, click to select the app for which you want to delete files, then click to select the document to delete in the Documents list.

2. Press the Delete button on your keyboard.

   iTunes displays an alert asking if you are sure you want to remove the item from your iPad.

3. Click Delete.

   The file will be deleted immediately, and will no longer appear in Keynote's Import Presentation window.

To import presentation documents using email:

1. On your computer, compose an email to an email address that is set up in the Mail app on your iPad. Attach a Keynote or PowerPoint file to the email and then send it.

2. On the iPad, launch the Mail app and select the received email message **C**.

   The attachment appears at the bottom of the email's message body.

3. Tap the attachment's icon.

   The presentation appears in a preview view **D**; this view is generated by the Mail app. The slides in the presentation will appear as pages; you can scroll through them. The preview has a toolbar at the top of the screen that disappears after a couple of seconds, allowing you to view the entire slide.

C In Mail on your iPad, display the email with the attached presentation file, then tap on the attachment.

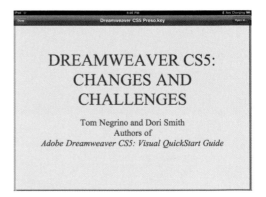

D Mail's preview of the document has the toolbar that disappears after a few seconds; tap the screen to bring the toolbar back.

E In the popover, tap Keynote to import the attached file into Keynote.

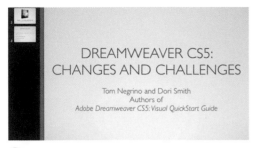

F After import, you can begin work on the presentation immediately.

G In Keynote for Mac, you can invite people to share the presentation on iWork.com.

H In iPad's Mail app, you get the invitation from iWork.com.

4. To move the presentation into Keynote, tap anywhere on the screen to bring back the toolbar, then at the right side of the toolbar, tap the Open in button.

   A popover appears showing the programs on your iPad that can read the presentation file **E**.

5. Tap Keynote.

   Keynote launches, imports the file, and displays it in the editing view **F**.

TIP Notice that the fonts are different between **D** and **F**. The correct fonts are in **F**, corresponding to the fonts used in the original Keynote for Mac file. So don't worry if the Mail preview shows you a distorted preview of the presentation; Keynote does a better job of rendering the presentation.

To import documents from iWork.com:

1. In Keynote '09 on the Mac, choose Share > Share via iWork.com.

   A dialog appears asking for information about who you want to share the file with, and allowing you to set sharing options **G**.

2. Fill out the sharing dialog, with yourself in the To field. The dialog creates an email message that will be sent to your email address on your iPad.

3. Click Share.

   You'll receive an email notifying you that there is a shared document waiting **H**.

continues on next page

---

4. In the email, tap Shared Documents.

If you haven't previously done so, you'll need to sign into your iWork.com account on your iPad . When you've done so, the Shared Documents view appears .

5. For the presentation you want, tap the blue button with the downward pointing arrow. From the list of file formats, choose Keynote '09.

A preview of the presentation appears .

6. Tap Open in Keynote.

Keynote launches, imports the file, and displays it in the editing view.

I If you haven't been there before on your iPad, you must sign into iWork.com.

J In the Shared Documents view, you can choose from a variety of formats to download the presentation file.

K Safari has its own preview. Tap the Open in Keynote button to import the file into Keynote.

A If you try to import an older Keynote file, Keynote for iPad registers its objection.

Folder button

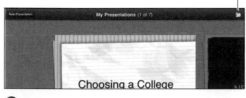

B Begin importing documents into Keynote by tapping the Folder button in the My Presentations view.

C The files from iTunes appear in the Import Presentation window.

Importing Keynote and PowerPoint Documents

Once you have your files on the iPad, it's time to actually import them into Keynote. The file formats Keynote for iPad can read are Keynote '09, PowerPoint 2007 and later (.pptx and .ppsx), and PowerPoint 97-2004 (.ppt and .pps). Keynote presentations created with older versions of iWork won't import successfully into Keynote for iPad. If you try, the program pops up an error window **A**.

Once on the iPad, the items in the Documents list in iTunes aren't yet in Keynote, but they can be accessed from Keynote's My Presentations view. In that view, tap the folder button at the right side of the toolbar **B** and the Import Presentation window appears **C**. The files in this window correspond to the files in the iTunes Documents list.

Once you are done importing a file into Keynote, the program makes an entirely separate new copy of the file, so you might want to delete the source file from the Import Presentation window. It's important to understand that the files in My Presentations and in Import Presentation are completely independent. The files you can browse through in My Presentations are Keynote files that you have either created in Keynote on the iPad or files that you have previously imported into Keynote using the Import Presentation window. If you happen to have files with the same name in My Presentations and Import Presentation, changes you make in Keynote *only* affect the copy of the file available in My Presentations.

To import documents into Keynote:

1. Launch Keynote on the iPad.

2. If you're not already there, tap the My Presentations button in Keynote's toolbar to switch to the My Presentations view **B**.

3. Tap the folder button at the right side of the toolbar, and the Import Presentation window appears **C**.

4. Tap one of the presentations in the Import Presentation list. If necessary, you can scroll the list to show more choices.

Keynote displays a progress bar while it is importing your file, then opens the file, ready to be edited (or presented, if it needs no changes) **D**.

In many cases, Keynote will display a window listing aspects of the original presentation that didn't import correctly (see the "Importing Limitations" section later in this chapter for more information).

TIP The PowerPoint file formats are interchangeable between the Windows and Macintosh versions of PowerPoint.

TIP Despite what it says in **D**, I am not a college director of admissions.

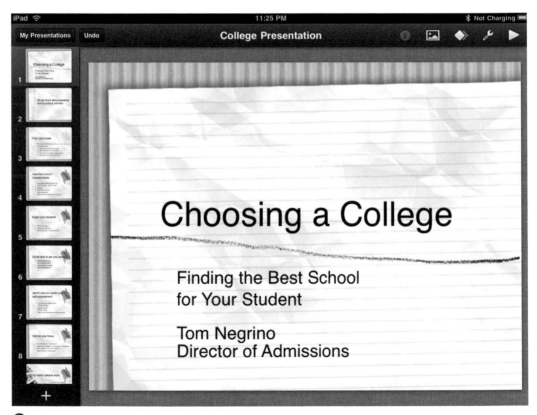

D After you import, Keynote prepares the file for any tweaking you might want to make.

E To choose a file for deletion, tap its red minus icon.

F Tap the red Delete confirmation button to erase the file from your iPad.

To delete documents from the Import Presentation window:

1. In Keynote, switch to the My Presentations view.

2. Tap the folder button at the right side of the toolbar, and the Import Presentation window appears **C**.

3. Tap the Edit button at the upper right corner of the window.

   The list of documents in the window changes to display a red minus icon appearing next to each document's name **E**.

4. Tap the red minus icon next to the document you want to delete.

   A red Delete confirmation button appears to the right of the document's name **F**.

5. Tap the Delete button.

   Keynote removes the file.

6. Tap the Done button at the upper right corner of the window **E**.

   The Import Presentation window changes back to its usual appearance.

7. Tap the Close button **C** to dismiss the window.

Importing Limitations

Keynote for iPad is a capable presentation program, but compared to Keynote on the Mac, it has a much smaller feature set. In general, if a feature in Keynote '09 isn't available in Keynote for iPad, aspects of your presentation that rely on the desktop version's features will be stripped out (and in some cases, completely discarded) when you import the presentation into Keynote for iPad. If you've been using Keynote for some time on the Mac, and have added fancy (or even some mundane) effects to your presentations, it can be disconcerting when you first import and open those presentations on the iPad.

Upon import of presentations with features that Keynote for iPad doesn't support, the program puts up a window letting you know what problems it encountered **A**. Unfortunately, this is often not a comprehensive list.

One of the biggest issues is simply that the iPad supports a limited selection of fonts (and you can't add your own), so unsupported fonts in your presentation are replaced with a font that Keynote considers to be a close match. If it can't find one, Keynote replaces the font with Helvetica.

You can find a list of iPad's fonts, as well as many other potential import issues, in this Apple Support article, "Keynote for iPad: Frequently Asked Questions": **http://support.apple.com/kb/HT4066**.

In tests, I discovered many aspects of Keynote and PowerPoint presentations that don't translate to Keynote for iPad. This list is representative, not complete:

Presentation Import Warnings
Keynote doesn't support some aspects of the original presentation.
All presenter notes were removed.
Grouped objects were ungrouped.
Builds on grouped objects were removed.

A When you import a presentation, Keynote tries to alert you to potential problems.

B Some aspects of a Keynote '09 file won't translate well when imported to the iPad. This is the identical slide on the Mac (above) and the iPad (below). The white background of the New Zealand map, which was knocked out using the Mac's Instant Alpha feature, reappears on the iPad. The Mac slide also uses a Smart Build to display several photos in an automatic sequence; all but the last of the photos were thrown away on the iPad.

- If you used a presentation theme that isn't built into Keynote for iPad (created by Apple or by third-party theme makers), any extra slide masters that theme contains will not be copied to the iPad; you're limited to Keynote's eight slide layouts. The unsupported theme's slide backgrounds will be imported as an image laid over Keynote's White theme.

- Grouped objects will become ungrouped. Sometimes, the objects in the group will be shifted.

- Presenter Notes and Comments are not imported.

- Some of the desktop version's slide transitions and builds are not supported. Unsupported transitions or builds will become a simple dissolve.

- Motion paths will not be imported.

- Action Builds and Smart Builds will be removed. If you have multiple photos in a Smart Build, only the last one will be imported.

- Graphics that had their background removed with the Instant Alpha feature will import with the original background **B**.

- Movies are supported, but embedded or recorded audio aren't imported.

- 3D charts are converted to 2D charts.

- You can't use hyperlinks to change to different slides (or to a browser) during the presentation.

So with all these issues, should you just throw up your hands in horror? Well, probably not. But before you present, you should review existing presentations, and if need be, revise them to suit the iPad environment.

continues on next page

Apple has another Support document with some good advice, called "Keynote for iPad: Best practices for creating a presentation on a Mac for use on an iPad." You can find it at **http://support.apple.com/ kb/HT4114**. The article lists recommended themes for Keynote for Mac that will translate to the iPad, and makes suggestions for handling images.

TIP **If you import a Keynote file that used an unsupported feature (which will be stripped out during import), make changes, then export them back to your Mac, you'll discover the original features will be gone. For example, Presenter Notes are eliminated altogether. Interestingly, PowerPoint files that are exported out of Keynote on the iPad retain at least some of their features, like motion paths, that don't translate into Keynote for iPad.**

Creating
a Presentation

A Keynote document includes all of the items that make up your presentation, including text, images, and dynamic media such as QuickTime movies. It also includes the set of *slide layouts* for the presentation. Slide layouts are templates for slides that you can use throughout your presentation. Slide layouts contain slide backgrounds and boxes for text and graphics that you'll fill in with your show's content. Slide layouts help your presentation look more polished and consistent. A group of slide layouts makes up a *theme*, the basic building block of a Keynote presentation.

In this chapter, you'll learn how to choose a theme for your presentation; add and organize slides; and learn how to manage and preview your presentations.

In This Chapter

Creating a New Presentation

When you start Keynote, the program, as with most iOS programs, assumes that you want to resume what you were doing when you last left the program. So, if you were editing a presentation, you'll go back to the same slide within that presentation. If you were last in the My Presentations view, you will return there. In any event, you begin creating a presentation in My Presentations.

All Keynote presentations begin with a theme. A theme provides a set of slide layouts and a graphic look for a presentation. Think of a theme as a template from which you can build your presentation. When you first create a Keynote document, you must choose a theme.

It's All About the Words

The most important part of your presentation is your message. All of Keynote's beautiful themes, slick graphics, and fancy transitions won't save your presentation if you don't have anything compelling to say. The presentation is *you*, not your visual aids.

Think of it this way: when you give a presentation, you're telling your audience a story. You know about stories; you've seen and heard thousands of them over the years, from movies, television, and real life. So you already know the most important thing about stories: they have to be interesting. If your story isn't, you'll lose your audience. And good stories begin with good, clear writing.

A good story has a conflict between characters or situations. In the course of the story, the conflict is resolved and the story ends. Good presentations hook audiences with a problem and then show how to deal with the problem. When the problem is resolved, the presentation is done.

Spend the bulk of your time writing your presentation, making sure that the message is strong and you're telling a compelling story. Then—and only then—work on the look of your presentation, including adding graphics, tables, and charts (if your talk needs them at all).

To create a new presentation:

1. Launch Keynote, and if you're not already there, go to the My Presentations view by tapping the My Presentations button in the toolbar.

   The My Presentations view appears **A**.

2. Tap the New Presentation button at the left edge of the toolbar.

   or

   Tap the New Presentation button at the bottom of the screen (the button with the plus (+) icon).

   The Choose a Theme view appears **B**.

3. Pick one of the available themes by tapping it.

continues on next page

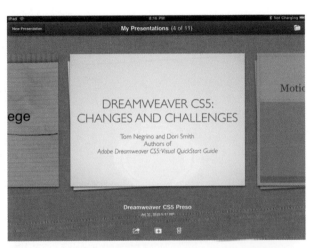

A You create new presentations in the My Presentations view.

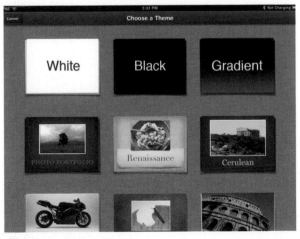

B Pick a theme that suits the style you want for your presentation.

Keynote creates the presentation and opens it in the editing view, displaying the first slide, using the Title, Subtitle & Photo slide layout 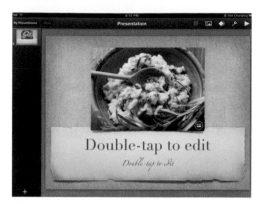. Some of the themes correspond to themes found in Keynote '09, but others do not. See the "Themes Comparison" sidebar.

C After you've created a presentation, it appears in the editing view, with the first slide (which is always a Title, Subtitle, & Photo slide) ready for editing.

Themes Comparison

Keynote for iPad (at least version 1.1, which is what I'm using for this book), comes with 12 presentation themes from which to choose. Some of these themes correspond almost exactly with themes built-in to Keynote '09, though most differ in subtle ways, and a couple are completely different.

According to Apple's support document, "Best practices for creating a presentation on a Mac for use on an iPad," found at **http://support.apple.com/kb/HT4114**, it's best to start on the Mac with one of the themes that correspond to a similar theme on the iPad, and also to set the slide size to 1024 × 768.

Keynote for iPad	Keynote '09
Theme	**Theme**
Black	Black
Chalkboard	Blackboard
Craft	Craft
Gradient	Gradient
Harmony	Harmony
Modern Portfolio	Modern Portfolio
Cerulean	Moroccan
Parchment	Parchment
Photo Portfolio	No similar theme
Renaissance	No similar theme
Showroom	Showroom
White	White

Adding Slides

Once you have created a presentation and applied a theme, you'll want to add additional slides. You'll use each different sort of slide layout for a particular purpose in your show. For example, the default slide layout type for the beginning of a presentation is Title, Subtitle, & Photo, which gives you a large line of type for the

presentation's title, centered horizontally on the slide. Underneath is a smaller line of type for a subtitle, if you want one. There is also a large photo placeholder to illustrate your presentation's topic.

You should become familiar with the eight slide layout types, as described in **Table 3.1** (on the next page). Keynote for iPad offers eight slide layouts for each theme **Ⓐ**.

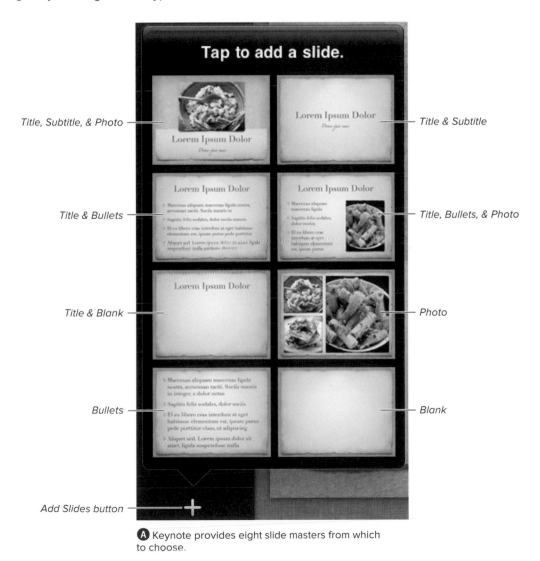

Title, Subtitle, & Photo

Title & Subtitle

Title & Bullets

Title, Bullets, & Photo

Title & Blank

Photo

Bullets

Blank

Add Slides button

Ⓐ Keynote provides eight slide masters from which to choose.

To add slides:

1. Tap the Add Slides button at the lower left corner of the editing area.

   The Tap to add a slide popover appears Ⓐ.

2. Tap the slide layout you want.

   Keynote adds the slide, and it appears in both the Slide Navigator and in the Slide Canvas.

   See Chapter 4 for more about working with text on slides and Chapter 5 for details on working with graphics.

TABLE 3.1 Slide Layout Types

Type	Description
Title, Subtitle, & Photo	By default, the first slide in a presentation.
Title & Subtitle	An alternate opening slide, lacking a photo placeholder.
Title & Bullets	Includes two text boxes. Top text box uses large type for the slide title; bottom text box uses smaller, bulleted text for body material.
Title, Bullets, & Photo	Contains a title box at the top of the slide, a text box for bulleted text below and to the left, and a photo placeholder below and to the right.
Title & Blank	Includes one text box with large type, justified to the top of the slide. Blank area below is often used for a large table or chart.
Photo	Contains one or more photo placeholders.
Bullets	Includes one text box with bulleted text for body material.
Blank	Contains only the slide background. Use this for really large or complex graphics.

Deleting Slides

Deleting unwanted slides is easy; just select the slide and get rid of it.

To delete slides:

1. In the Slide Navigator, slow double-tap the slide you want to delete.

   The Edit popover appears **A**.

2. Tap Delete.

   The slide disappears.

TIP If you accidentally delete a slide, immediately tap the Undo button in the toolbar.

TIP If you delete the first slide in a group of slides (see "Grouping Slides" later in this chapter), all the slides indented below it will also be deleted. Be careful!

A Tap the Delete button to remove the selected slide from your presentation.

Grouping Slides

In the Slide Navigator, Keynote allows you to organize your presentation by indenting related slides. Indenting slides in this way doesn't change the final presentation. It's a tool that helps you organize large sets of slides.

Once you have grouped related slides together, you can show or hide groups to make it easier for you to work with and organize the presentation.

To group slides:

1. In the Slide Navigator, tap to select a slide you wish to indent.

2. Tap and drag the slide to the right.

   The slide is indented, and a disclosure triangle appears next to the slide above the indented slide **A**.

3. Repeat as necessary until you have indented all the slides that you want.

To hide and show slide groups:

Tap the disclosure triangle next to the first slide in the group to hide a group of slides, as shown in **B**. Tap the disclosure triangle again to show the slides in the group.

TIP You can select multiple slides in the Slide Navigator by tapping the first slide in the group to select it, and then holding one finger on that slide while tapping other slides with another finger.

TIP If you have multiple slides selected, you can drag them all at once.

TIP You can outdent slides (i.e., move slides that were previously indented to the left) by electing one or more slides in the Slide Navigator and dragging to the left.

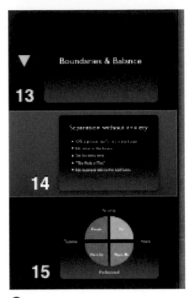

A Slides 14 and 15 are grouped under slide 13.

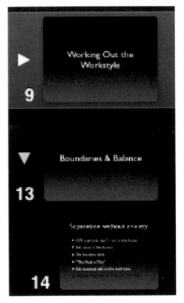

B With the group hidden, you can't see slides 10 through 12 in the Slide Navigator.

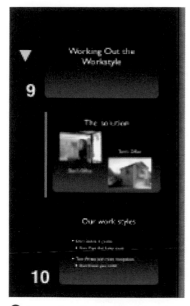

A A gray line shows where the slide will move when released.

Changing the Slide Order

The Slide Navigator also allows you to rearrange the slides in your presentation, by dragging the slide's thumbnail up or down in the Slide Navigator.

There are times when you have your presentation ready to go, and you arrive at the venue and realize that you don't want to show some of the slides in your presentation. Perhaps your company's product line has changed, and you want to hide the slide that shows the fabulous Wonder Widget because it will soon be replaced by a new model (probably the Ultra Wonder Widget). Sometimes even news reports are a reason to remove slides from your presentation; for example, you probably wouldn't have wanted to give a presentation with a picture of a sinking ship the day after the *Titanic* went down.

To rearrange slides:

1. Select the slide that you wish to move.

2. Drag it up or down in the Slide Navigator.

   A gray line appears, indicating where the slide will go when you release the slide **A**.

To move slide groups:

Select the first slide in the group and drag the group up or down in the Slide Navigator. A gray line appears in the Slide Navigator to show where the slides will be placed.

To skip slides:

1. In the Slide Navigator, slow double-tap the slide that you want to skip.

   The Edit popover appears **B**.

2. Tap Skip.

   Keynote collapses the thumbnail image of the slide in the Slide Navigator to a line **C**.

TIP To restore a skipped slide in your pre-sentation, slow double-tap the collapsed slide thumbnail in the Slide Navigator, and choose Don't Skip from the resulting Edit popover.

B The Edit popover appears, with the Skip option.

C After selecting a slide in the Slide Navigator and setting it to be skipped, Keynote shows the slide as a line and renumbers subse-quent slides.

Duplicating Slides

Why might you want to duplicate a slide? The most common reason is that you have added some custom elements to a slide— such as a graphic or a custom text box— that you want to appear on a few slides, and don't want to have to recreate again and again.

To duplicate slides:

1. Slow double-tap on the slide you want to duplicate.

   The Edit popover appears.

2. Tap Copy.

3. (Optional) Scroll the Slide Navigator to where you want the duplicated slide to appear.

4. Slow double-tap on a slide in the Slide Navigator.

5. Tap Paste.

   The duplicated slide appears in the Slide Navigator.

Managing Presentations

Presentation management occurs in the My Presentations view. You can duplicate, rename, or delete any presentation in that view.

To duplicate an existing presentation:

1. In the My Presentations view, center the presentation you want to duplicate.

2. Below the centered presentation, tap the New Presentation button.

   A popover appears **A**.

3. Tap Duplicate Presentation.

   Keynote creates a duplicate of the presentation, named "*Presentation* copy," and centers the duplicate in the My Presentations view.

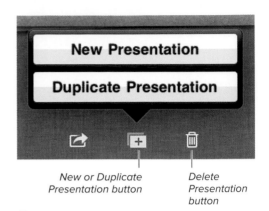

New or Duplicate
Presentation button

Delete
Presentation
button

A Tap to duplicate the existing presentation.

To rename a presentation:

1. In the My Presentations view, center the presentation you want to rename.

2. Tap the name of the presentation.

   Keynote makes the name editable **B**.

3. Type the new name for the presentation.

4. Tap the Done button in the toolbar, or tap anywhere other than on the presentation's name.

TIP If you have an external keyboard attached to your iPad, the on-screen keyboard will not appear.

To delete a presentation:

1. In the My Presentations view, center the presentation you want to delete.

2. Tap the Delete Presentation button.

   A confirmation popover appears **C**.

3. Tap Delete Presentation.

B Enter the new name for the presentation.

C Tap to confirm the presentation's deletion.

Numbering Slides

If you prefer (most of the time, I do not, because I don't think it adds to most presentations), you can have a number appear on each slide. Slide numbering in Keynote for iPad is an all-or-nothing proposition. Turning it on makes unobtrusive numbers appear on every slide (yes, including the first slide). These slide numbers are not editable in any way.

To number slides:

1. In the editing view, tap the Tools button in the toolbar **A**.

2. In the resulting popover, tap the switch next to Slide Numbers so that it shows On.

   Keynote adds the numbers to the slide **B**. The exact position and appearance depends on the presentation's theme.

A Tap the Slide Numbers switch on.

B Slide numbers appear at the bottom of each slide.

Play button

Ⓐ Tap Play to begin your run-through.

Previewing the Presentation

When you're done creating your presentation, it's often useful to run it through as
a slideshow once or twice. This helps you
get a feel for the flow of the presentation
and almost always shows you places where
the presentation could use tightening or
better explanation.

After you run the slideshow, you can return
to individual slides to tweak the text, or
you can begin adding graphics, tables, and
charts to your presentation.

To run your presentation:

1. In the Slide Navigator, tap the first slide
   in the presentation.

2. Tap the Play button in the toolbar Ⓐ.

   The slideshow begins. Tap anywhere
   on the screen to advance through
   your slides.

3. To end the slideshow, double-tap anywhere on the screen, and Keynote will
   return to the editing view.

4

Getting the Type Right

In general, I think that you should write your presentation before you ever start working with Keynote. Even writing your topics for each slide on a piece of paper first will help. Focusing on your presentation's text, rather than the text on your individual slides, will lead you to create better presentations.

But sooner or later, you will need to work with the text on your slides, and that's what this chapter is all about. For this chapter, at least, I'll assume that you'll be entering text directly onto slides.

Keynote showcases iOS's superior text handling, layout, and display abilities, and you've got good control over the appearance and style of text within Keynote.

In this chapter, you'll learn how to enter text on slides, style that text as you wish, change the alignment and spacing of text, work with indents on slides, save time when you're setting text styles, and avoid embarrassing spelling errors.

In This Chapter

Adding Title and Body Text

The first slide in your presentation is by default the Title, Subtitle, & Photo slide (though you can delete and replace it if you want), which contains three pieces of information: the title of the presentation; a subtitle, where you put your name and company affiliation; and a photo place-holder, to illustrate the overall topic of your presentation Ⓐ.

In Keynote, all text must be in *text boxes*. A text box defines the boundaries of the text. If you have more text than the text box can contain (which depends on the size of the text box and the size and style of the text within the box), Keynote first shrinks the text size, trying to make the extra text fit. If you persist in adding text to the text box, text will be cut off, and Keynote will display a plus icon at the bottom of the text box to let you know that you are missing some text. Text automatically wraps inside text boxes.

Most of the time, you'll use the text boxes provided on the slide layout that you have chosen for your slide, but you can also add your own text boxes to a particular slide, as discussed in the next section.

Photo placeholder

Title text box

Subtitle text box

Ⓐ By default, the first slide of any new presentation uses the Title, Subtitle, & Photo slide layout.

To add title and body text:

1. Create a new presentation file, and apply a theme from the "Choose a Theme" view.

   Keynote creates a new slide based on the Title, Subtitle, & Photo slide layout. The new slide will contain placeholder text for its text boxes, which say, "Double-tap to edit," as shown in Ⓐ.

2. Double-tap in the title box, which usually contains larger sized text than the subtitle.

   An insertion point will begin blinking in the title box.

3. Type in your title using the on-screen keyboard, or, if you have one, an external keyboard.

4. When you're done entering the title, tap outside the title box to deselect it, or double-tap in the subtitle box to begin entering your subtitle.

   You'll know Keynote's ready for you to enter text in the subtitle box when you see the insertion point blinking in that box.

5. Type in your subtitle Ⓑ.

6. Tap outside the subtitle box to deselect it.

TIP It's natural to want to press Return or Enter when you're done entering text in a Keynote text box. But if you do that, Keynote will insert another line in the text box.

TIP Your default title slide has a photo placeholder. See Chapter 5 for information about placing graphics on slides.

Ⓑ Double-tap to replace the text placeholders and enter text on slides.

Working with Text Boxes

On many slides, you'll use *bulleted text*, which you've seen in most presentations to denote the individual talking points on a slide **A**. Bulleted text is just that, text preceded by a marker called a bullet. In Keynote, a bullet can be either a text character or an image built into the theme. When you enter text in a bulleted text box, Keynote automatically inserts the bullets whenever you begin a new line by pressing Return.

To enter bulleted text:

1. Create a slide with a slide layout containing a bulleted text box.

   Typical slide layouts with bulleted text boxes include Title & Bullets, Bullets, and Title, Bullets & Photo.

2. In the text box with the "Double-tap to edit" placeholder, double-tap to place the insertion point.

3. Enter your text.

   If your entry is too large for the text box, it will wrap within the text box, with the default left text alignment.

4. Press Return to begin a new line.

   Keynote automatically inserts a new bullet at the beginning of the line.

TIP In every other presentation program on the planet (OK, that could be a bit of hyperbole), including Keynote for Mac, you indent text one level in a bulleted text box by pressing Tab before you begin typing on a new line. But there's no Tab key on the on-screen iOS keyboard. So bulleted text is just a list style. To indent text, see "Setting Text Alignment and Spacing," and for information about working with lists, see "Working with Lists," both later in this chapter.

Healdsburg: the best of the wine country

▷ Wine - at the intersection of three of the finest wine growing appellations in the world

▷ Food - everything from neighborhood taquerias to Michelin-starred restaurants

▷ Friends - you'll meet old and make new

▷ Fun - bicycling, shopping, enjoying live music, or just hanging out by the Russian River

A This text box contains all the bullets on your slide.

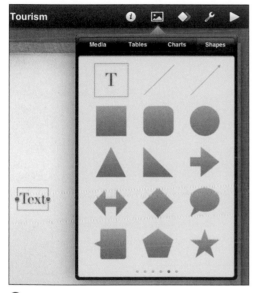

B You can use a free text box as a picture caption.

C Tap the big T in the Shapes pane of the Media popover to add a free text box, which you can see on the slide.

Adding Text Boxes

Besides the bulleted text boxes found on many slide layouts, you can also add your own text boxes to slides. These "free" text boxes can be used wherever you need extra text on a slide. For example, you can use a free text box as a picture caption **B**.

To add a free text box:

1. On the slide where you want to add the text box, tap the Media button on the toolbar.

   The Media popover appears **C**. Tapping one of the items in this popover places it on the slide canvas. There are four panes in the popover: Media, Tables, Charts, or Shapes. The popover appears displaying the pane you last used.

2. If necessary, tap the Shapes button in the popover to get to the correct pane, and then tap the Text item in the popover (the big T).

   A text box appears in the center of the slide with the placeholder text "Text" **C**.

3. Drag the text box to where you want to position it on the slide.

   As you drag the text box, Keynote will show you alignment guides (shown as yellow lines on the slide) to help you line the text up easily.

4. Double-tap in the text box to get an insertion point and then enter your text.

> **TIP** Free text boxes only have two selection handles, at the right and left edges. Free text boxes automatically grow or shrink vertically to handle the length of your text. They can't be made taller by dragging.

> **TIP** If you don't see the alignment guides as you move objects on the slide, they are turned off in the Guides section of the Tools popover.

Styling Text

One of the benefits of Keynote's themes and slide layouts is that much of the work of styling is done for you. In many cases, you won't have any need to style slide text, even though you have a complete style toolbox available to you.

But when you want to style text in Keynote, it's important to know that the program acts differently depending on whether you have selected a text box (which contains text), or you have selected text that is inside a text box. In either case, you make your changes by tapping the Info button in the toolbar, but the available options differ based on your selection, as shown in **Table 4.1**.

TABLE 4.1 Style Options

Text box selected	Individually selected text

Style
■ Preset styles
■ Style options
  ▸ Fill
  ▸ Border
  ▸ Effects
    • Shadow
    • Opacity
	Style
	■ Bold, Italic, Underline, Strikethrough
	■ Preset styles
	■ Text options
	  ▸ Size
	  ▸ Color
	  ▸ Font

Text
■ Bold, Italic, Underline, Strikethrough
■ Preset styles
■ Text options
  ▸ Size
  ▸ Color
  ▸ Font
  ▸ Alignment
  ▸ Inset margin
	List
	■ Indent/Outdent
	■ List types
	  ▸ Bullets
	  ▸ Image
	  ▸ Lettered
	  ▸ Numbered

Arrange ■ Move to back/front	**Layout** ■ Alignment ■ Inset margin ■ Columns ■ Line spacing

When you have a whole text box selected, the Info popover looks like **A**. When you select text within a text box, the popover looks like **B**.

Keynote treats text boxes as a special kind of graphic, so two of the sections in Table 4.1 (*Style* and *Arrange*, under Text box selected) work much the same as they do for any graphic. I'll address how those sections work in Chapter 5, when I discuss working with graphics. Styling all the text in a text box (*Text*, under Text box selected) works almost the same as when you have individual text selected; the only change is that some of the controls are in different places.

Keynote also treats hyperlinks in a different fashion than other text. Keynote automatically formats the text when you type a Web address into a slide, such as **www.peachpit. com**. Keynote is smart enough to automatically turn that into a hyperlink, and it can also handle email addresses **C**.

> **TIP** If you're playing the presentation on the iPad screen, you can tap a hyperlink during your presentation, which leaves Keynote and hides it, opens Safari or Mail, and brings you to the hyperlink's destination. But if you're displaying the presentation on an external screen, you can't activate the hyperlink.

B The Style pane of the Info popover when you have text on a slide selected.

Contact Us!

> Web: www.healdsburg.com
> Email: info@healdsburg.com

C Keynote knows how to automatically format Web and e-mail addresses on slides.

Copying Styles

Sometimes, rather than recreating a set of styles from scratch, it's enough to say that you want *this* text to look like *that* text over there. Keynote makes it easy to copy text styles from one place to another. When you copy styles, Keynote replicates the whole set of styles from the source, including the font, size, text color, and so on, to the target text.

To copy styles:

1. Select the source text, which has the style you want to copy.

   The Edit popover appears 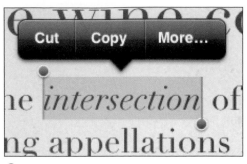.

2. Tap More.

   The Edit popover changes **E**.

3. Tap Copy Style.

4. Select the target text, to which you want to copy the style.

   The Edit popover appears.

5. Tap More.

   The More choices appear in the Edit popover **F**.

6. Tap Paste Style.

   The selected text takes on the styles of the source text.

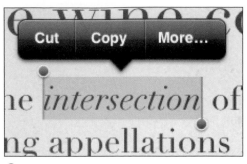

D Begin copying styles with the Edit popover.

E Tapping the Edit popover's More button displays the Copy Style choice.

F Tap Paste Style to apply the copied style to the selected text.

Working with
Font Styles

Keynote does a great job of showing off the excellent font capabilities of the iPad. The operating system comes with a good selection of razor-sharp fonts, and Keynote lets you display them to best effect. You can scale text with no loss of quality, so your presentations remain readable (unless you make the text too small for people in the back row!).

Keynote has the concept of *preset text styles*, which are part of the theme file, and allow you to apply a number of styling options with a single tap. Of course, if you prefer, you can add any style attributes you like, one at a time. Unfortunately, there's no way to create your own preset text styles.

Remember that depending on what you have selected, you can control the styling either for an entire text box, or for selected text within a text box. Text styling when you select a text box is available by tapping the Info button in the toolbar, and then tapping the button to display the Text pane in the resulting popover. Settings within this pane are almost identical to the settings in Info > Style when you've selected text within a text box. Because this chapter is about working with text, the instructions in this section focus on text within a text box.

To apply preset text styles:

1. Select the text you want to change.

2. Tap the Info button in the toolbar.

   The popover appears. If necessary, tap the Style button to display the Style pane 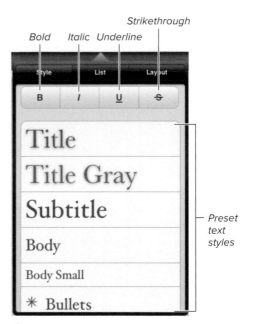.

3. To make the text bold, italic, underlined, or strikethrough, tap the respective button at the top of the popover. You can apply more than one of these options if you like.

   or

   Tap on one of the preset text styles. This list scrolls to show more available styles; swipe up to show them.

   Keynote styles the text.

To change text size, color, or font:

1. Select the text you want to change.

2. Tap the Info button in the toolbar.

   The popover appears. If necessary, tap the Style button to display the Style pane Ⓐ.

3. Swipe up to display the bottom of the popover, and then tap Text Options.

   The Text Options pane appears Ⓑ.

Ⓐ You'll use the Style pane of the Info popover to style selected text.

Ⓑ The Text Options pane allows you to change the font size, color, or font family.

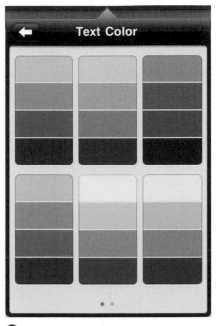

C Tap on a swatch to apply that color to the selected text.

4. To change the text's size, tap the up or down arrows in the size widget.

   or

   To change the text color, tap the color swatch, which displays the Text Color pane **C**. Swipe as needed to see all the color options. Tap the one you want and then tap the arrow in the title bar to return to Text Options.

   or

   To change the font, tap Font, which displays the Fonts pane **D**. Swipe to scroll the list, and then tap the font you want. To display the different typefaces for a font family, tap the arrow next to the name of the font family and then tap the typeface **E**.

Fonts

Helvetica ❯
Helvetica Neue ❯
Hiragino Kaku Gothic⋯ ❯
Hiragino Mincho ProN⋯ ❯
✓ Hoefler Text ❯
Marker Felt Wide ❯
Optima Regular ❯
Palatino ❯
Papyrus ❯

D Choose the font family you want from the Fonts pane.

Helvetica

Regular ✓
Light
Oblique
Light Oblique
Bold
Bold Oblique

E A given font family may have many typefaces, only a few, or just one.

Working with Lists

Keynote treats bulleted text as a kind of list, and gives you full control over that list's indentation, limited control over the kind of bullets it uses (text bullets or a single kind of image bullet built into the theme), and whether letters or numbers automatically precede items in the list. You can't mix different bullet styles within a text box, but you can set some items in the list to have no bullets, as shown in Ⓐ.

To change text indentation:

1. Select the text you want to change.

2. Tap the Info button in the toolbar.

   The popover appears. If necessary, tap the List button to display the List pane Ⓑ.

3. To indent text (shift it to the right), tap the Indent button.

   or

   To outdent text (shift it to the left), tap the Outdent button.

   The text moves as you command.

TIP When working with lists, don't forget that you can select multiple lines and change them all at once.

Ⓐ All of the items in this text box started off with bullets, but I individually selected the program names and selected None from the bullet choices.

Ⓑ You indent or outdent text using the List pane.

1. Mercury
- Freedom 7 - first suborbital flight
- Friendship 7 - first orbital flight
2. Gemini
- Gemini IV - first space walk
- Gemini IX - first rendezvous and docking
3. Apollo
- Apollo 8 - first lunar orbit
- Apollo 11 - first lunar landing
- Apollo 17 - final lunar mission

C Sometimes the easiest way to get what you want is simply to type it, rather than try to make automatic numbering work.

To use text or image bullets:

1. Select the text you want to change.
2. Tap the Info button in the toolbar.

   The popover appears. If necessary, tap the List button to display the List pane.
3. To use a text bullet, tap Bullets.

   or

   To use an image bullet, tap Image.

   The selected text changes to the bullet style you set.

TIP You can see what either a text or image bullet will look like in the popover, to the left of each label. Unfortunately, Keynote for iPad doesn't allow you to set custom image bullets, as you can with Keynote '09.

TIP You can make text more important on your slide by increasing its size and setting the bullet to None **A**.

TIP You can work around Keynote's inability to mix different kinds of bullets. I wanted to number the different space programs, so I just typed the numbers in before each program name **C**. It's inelegant, but it works.

To set lettered or numbered lists:

1. Select the text you want to change.
2. Tap the Info button in the toolbar.

   The popover appears. If necessary, tap the List button to display the List pane.
3. To set the list to use letters, tap Lettered.

   or

   To set the list to use numbers, tap Numbered.

Setting Text Layout

Keynote has several controls for arranging text within a text box. You can set the text's alignment, left indent (Keynote calls this the *inset margin*), line spacing, and the number of columns the text flows into (which isn't— and shouldn't be—used on slides very often).

Keynote has two ways to control text alignment: horizontal and vertical. You can set horizontal alignment in the four standard ways: Left, Center, Right, and Justified. You can set vertical alignment, which controls where the text is placed (Top, Center, Bottom) within its text box.

To set text alignment:

1. On your slide, select the text whose alignment you wish to change.

2. Tap the Info button in the toolbar.

   The popover appears. If necessary, tap the Layout button to display the Layout pane **A**.

3. Tap the appropriate alignment button in the Alignment section.

   The text alignment changes.

To set the inset margin:

1. On your slide, select the text whose inset margin you wish to change.

2. Tap the Info button in the toolbar.

   The popover appears. If necessary, tap the Layout button to display the Layout pane **A**.

3. Drag the slider in the Inset Margin section.

   As you move the slider, the inset shows in points, on the right side of the section.

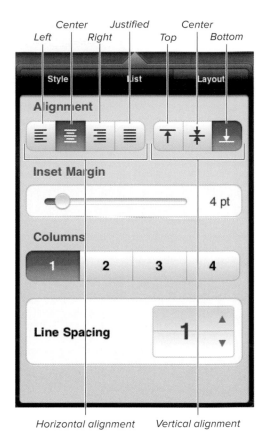

A Use the buttons in the List pane to set horizontal and vertical alignment.

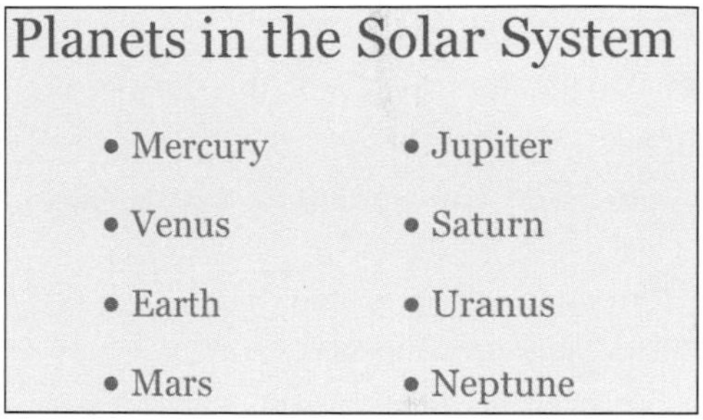

```
Planets in the Solar System

   • Mercury        • Jupiter

   • Venus          • Saturn

   • Earth          • Uranus

   • Mars           • Neptune
```

B The bulleted text has been set to appear as two columns.

To set the number of columns:

1. On your slide, select the text you want to put into columns.

2. Tap the Info button in the toolbar.

The popover appears. If necessary, tap the Layout button to display the Layout pane **A**.

3. In the Columns section, tap the number of columns you want.

The text changes **B**.

TIP Depending on the font styling you have set, you may need to drag the text box containing the columns of text on your slide to make it look centered, as I did in **B**.

To set the line spacing:

1. Select the text that you wish to change.

2. Tap the Info button in the toolbar.

The popover appears. If necessary, tap the Layout button to display the Layout pane.

3. In the Line Spacing section, tap the up or down arrows to increase or decrease the line spacing in ½ line increments.

Finding and Replacing Text

Keynote allows you to find, or find and replace text on your slides, which is handy when Marketing tells you that they've decided to rename the SuperWidget to UltraWidget half an hour before your presentation.

You can also replace text with a best guess from Keynote's dictionary, which is sometimes useful, but more often inadvertently hilarious.

To find or replace text:

1. Tap the Tools button in the toolbar, and then tap Find **A**.

   The Find popover appears at the bottom of the screen.

2. Type the word or phrase you want to find and press Return.

   Keynote finds the first instance of the text **B**.

A Begin finding text in the Tools popover.

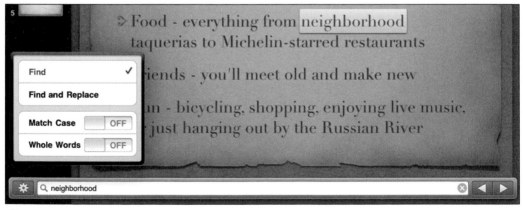

B Keynote highlights found text in yellow.

3. (Optional) If you want to replace the found text, tap the Settings button (it looks like a gear) at the left edge of the Find popover, tap Find & Replace, and then type the replacement text in the Replace field **C**. Tap Replace to change the text.

TIP Holding down the Replace button gives you a **Replace All** popover, which makes it easy to change text throughout your presentation.

TIP You can step through instances of found text with the arrow buttons at the right edge of the Find popover.

To replace text from the dictionary:

1. Select a word on a slide.

   The Edit popover appears.

2. Tap More.

   The More popover appears **D**.

3. Tap Replace.

   A popover appears with suggestions from Keynote's dictionary **E**.

4. Tap one of the suggestions to replace the selected text with the suggestion.

C Enter text you want to find in the left field, and text you want to replace it with in the right field.

D You'll find Replace after you tap More in the Edit popover.

E Choose a replacement (or not) from the choices Keynote offers.

Proofing your Work

By default, spell checking is turned on in Keynote, and misspellings will show up on your slides with red dotted underlines, as in any other iOS program.

To fix misspellings:

1. Tap on a word with a red dotted underline.

   The dotted underline goes away, and a suggestion popover appears with one or more suggestions **A**.

2. Tap the replacement you want.

   Keynote replaces the misspelled word.

> **TIP** You can turn spell checking off by changing the setting in the Tools popover (see **A** in "Finding and Replacing Text").

> **TIP** If you misspell a word to such an extent that Keynote has no suggestion, the popover will say "No Replacements Found."

Using the Dictionary

Keynote uses the iPad's built-in dictionary to give you definitions, which is useful for those times when you spell a word correctly, but still wonder, "Is that the right word in this context?" Wonder no more, my friend.

To use the dictionary:

1. Select a word on a slide.

   The Edit popover appears.

2. Tap More.

   The More popover appears (see **D** in "Finding and Replacing Text").

3. Tap Definition.

   The Dictionary popover appears, with the word's definition **B**.

A Tap the word you want from the suggestion popover.

B The definition of most of the words in your presentation is just a couple of taps away.

Illustrating Your Presentation

The text on your slides will usually carry the weight of your presentation, but the content can be greatly enhanced by the look of your slideshow. Much of that look is provided by the theme you select for your presentation. But graphics on the slide can also add zing to a professional-looking presentation, and often they contribute a significant part of the content of the presentation, as well.

In this chapter, you'll learn how to use Keynote—with the help of other graphics apps—to add and enhance graphics for your slides.

In This Chapter

Placing Images and Videos

The graphics on your slides will be one of two types: *imported graphics*, which include photographs and drawings from other graphic programs; and *shapes*, which are simple vector graphics that you can create within Keynote (more about shapes later in this chapter.)

Most presentations use photographs and clip art as illustrations, and three of Keynote's slide layouts (Title, Subtitle, & Photo, Title, Bullets, & Photo, and Photo)

have photo placeholders that are ready to accept graphics from the iPad's Photo Library **A**. The nice thing about using placeholders is that the photo drops into the placeholder, which acts as a window onto the photo, masking off parts of the photo you may not want to see. You can edit the mask, moving and scaling the photo under the mask (see Masking Images, later in this chapter).

You can also place images and videos from the Photo Library on slides without using a photo placeholder. In fact, you can't put a video into a photo placeholder.

Title, Subtitle, & Photo

Title, Bullets, & Photo

Photo

A Only three of Keynote's slide layouts come with photo placeholders.

To insert images into photo placeholders:

1. At the bottom of the Slide Navigator, tap the Plus button to display the slide layout popover, and then tap one of the layouts with a photo placeholder.

   or

   In the Slide Navigator, tap to display the existing slide you want to put the graphic on.

   A photo placeholder has a media button in its lower-right corner **B**.

continues on next page

Media buttons

B Photo placeholders have a Media button in their lower-right corners.

2. Tap the Media button in the placeholder to open the Photo Albums popover **C**.

   The contents of your iPad's Photo Library appear in the popover

3. Tap one of the albums in the popover to narrow your choices.

4. Tap the image you want.

   The image appears inside the photo placeholder on the slide **D**.

TIP You can almost always copy a graphic in another app, switch to Keynote, and paste the graphic into the slide.

C Tapping a Media button in a photo placeholder brings up the Photo Albums popover.

To place images:

1. Select the slide you want in the Slide Navigator.

2. Tap the Media button in the toolbar to open the Photo Albums popover **E**.

3. Tap one of the albums in the popover to narrow your choices.

4. Tap the image you want.

   The image appears on the slide.

D The new picture replaces the contents of the photo placeholder.

E To place photos on slides without using a photo placeholder, tap the Media button in the toolbar.

To place videos:

1. Select the slide you want in the Slide Navigator.

2. Tap the Media button in the toolbar to open the Photo Albums popover, and then tap the album that contains the video you want.

3. Tap the thumbnail of the video.

   The Choose Video pane appears **F**. You can preview the video by tapping the Play button below the video, or you can scrub through the video by dragging the playhead in the preview area above the video.

4. Tap Use.

   Keynote compresses the video for better playback, and then the video appears on the slide **G**.

> **TIP** An image or video that isn't in a placeholder will hardly ever be the right size or in the position you want. See "Positioning and Resizing Graphics" later in this chapter.

To delete graphics:

To delete a graphic or video, slow double-tap it and tap Delete in the resulting Edit popover.

Playhead

Preview area

Play button

F When you select a video in the Media popover, you can preview it before putting it on your slide.

G You can tap the Play button in the middle of the video to preview it in context on your slide.

Positioning and Resizing Graphics

Keynote treats graphics much like other slide objects. Once you have placed your image into Keynote, you will usually have to move it to just where you want it on the slide (if you didn't place it into a photo placeholder), and resize it in some way. That can mean scaling it (making it bigger or smaller) or cropping it (trimming the image to only the part you want). You can scale images in Keynote, but Keynote doesn't have the ability to crop an image. It does, however, have something even better, called masking (described in the next section).

To move graphics:

To move a graphic, you deal with it as you would any other slide object. Tap once on the graphic to select it, and then touch and drag to move it.

To resize graphics:

1. Select the image on your slide.

    Selection handles appear around the image **A**.

2. Touch and drag one of the handles to resize the object.

3. After you resize the object to your liking, it will probably not be in the correct position on the slide. Drag it to a position more to your liking.

A Drag selection handles to resize the image.

Selection handles

Using the Alignment Guides

Keynote's yellow alignment guides appear when you need them; you'll notice them appearing and disappearing as you move objects around the Slide Canvas **B**. The guides help you center and align objects on the canvas. The guides appear whenever the center or edge of an object aligns with the center or edge of another object, or with the center of the Slide Canvas. When the alignment guides appear, the object snaps to them.

You'll also see *position tags* that appear along with the guides. These tags display the X and Y coordinates of the top-left corner of each object as you move it around the Slide Canvas.

The position tag changes into an *angle tag* when you rotate a graphic object. You can do that by placing two fingers on the object, and then turning your hand **C**. When rotating, an alignment guide appears from the angle tag to the center of the object, and the object snaps to the guide at 45 degree increments.

Similarly, the position tag changes into a *size tag* when you resize a graphic **D**.

Position tags

x: -342 px y: -114 px

Alignment guides

B As you move an object on your slide, the yellow alignment guides appear.

C The angle tag appears when you rotate a graphic.

w: 410 px h: 307 px

D When you resize a graphic, the size tag appears.

Nudging Objects

Moving objects around on the canvas with your fingers can sometimes be imprecise; a stray twitch of a finger can move an object much further than you intended. Instead, you can move items in single-pixel increments by nudging them.

To nudge an object:

Touch and hold the object with one finger, and then use another finger, anywhere on the slide, to swipe in the direction you want the object to move.

A position tag appears, showing you the X and Y position on the canvas. As you swipe, you can see the position change in single-pixel increments.

Matching Object Sizes

Sometimes you want two images on a slide to be the same size. You can quickly match their sizes in Keynote.

To match two objects' sizes:

1. Select the object you want to resize, and then drag one of its selection handles.

2. With your other hand, touch and hold another object that has the size you want **E**.

3. When Keynote displays a tag that says Match Size, lift both fingers **F**.

   The first object resizes.

E The picture in front needs to be the same size as the picture in back.

F Lift your fingers when the Match Size tag appears.

A Double-tapping a photo makes the Mask slider appear.

B When you place the mask, areas of the image outside the mask area are dimmed.

Masking Images

As noted earlier, photo placeholders in Keynote act as masks, meaning that only part of the photo may be visible. You can think of a mask as a window through which part of the photo appears. You can resize the mask, or move or resize the image inside the mask.

When you place an image on a slide without a photo placeholder, you can still resize or reshape the image, and then use the new shape as the mask for the image.

1. Select an image on the slide.

2. Double-tap the image.

   The mask slider appears below the image A.

3. Drag the slider to make the image larger or smaller within the mask.

   The area of the image outside the mask is dimmed B.

4. Drag the mask's selection handles to resize the mask area. You can also touch and drag inside the mask area to reposition the image under the mask.

   You can even rotate the image within the mask by touching the image with two fingers and turning your hand.

5. To exit mask mode tap Done.

TIP If the image is inside a photo placeholder, and you want to restore the original mask, tap the Info button in the toolbar, tap Arrange, and then tap the Reset Mask button.

Inserting Shapes

Keynote's shapes are vector graphics that can be scaled and manipulated with no loss of resolution. Because Keynote's repertoire of shapes is limited (there are only 14: two kinds of lines, rectangle, rounded rectangle, oval, triangle, right triangle, arrow, double-headed arrow, diamond, two kinds of quote bubble, pentagon, and star), you'll probably be relying more on other graphics programs to provide complex slide graphics, and then importing them into Keynote via the iPad's Photo Library.

To place Keynote shapes:

1. In the Slide Navigator, tap to select the slide you want to put the shape on.

2. Tap the Media button on the toolbar, and then (if necessary), tap the Shapes button.

   The Shapes popover appears **A**. You can swipe right or left to display the shapes in different colors.

3. Tap the shape you want.

   The shape appears on the slide **B**. It is selected, so you can modify it. Some shapes have green control points that you can drag to reshape the object. For example, the quote bubble shapes have two control points. Dragging the top control point changes the bubble between an oval and a rectangle. Dragging the bottom control point changes the length and position of the quote bubble's "tail" **C**.

TIP Once you place a shape, you can't change it to a different kind of shape. For example, you can't convert a rectangle into a circle.

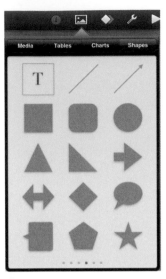

A You can swipe left or right in the Shapes popover to get different color options.

B Different shapes will have different numbers of selection handles.

C I've dragged the control point for this quote bubble to better indicate what my cat is thinking.

Ⓐ This text is embedded in the shape, moves with the shape, and rewraps as the shape is resized.

Inserting Text into Shapes

You can place text directly within shapes you've created in Keynote. The text that you add will be overlaid on the shape's fill. Text inside the shape rewraps as you resize the shape, and also as you resize the font size.

To add text to a shape:

1. Using the Media button on the toolbar, place a shape on the slide you're working with.

2. Resize the shape to your liking.

3. Double-tap in the middle of the shape. An insertion point will appear, centered in the shape.

4. Type the text you want in the shape **Ⓐ**.

TIP You can make the text adjustments available to any Keynote text by selecting the text within the shape, tapping the Info button in the toolbar, and then using the options in the resulting popover. See Chapter 4 for more information.

Styling Photos

Photos and shapes have different styling options. You can change the border around a photo, add a drop shadow, add a reflection effect, and change the photo's opacity.

To style photos:

1. Select the photo you wish to style.

2. Tap the Info button in the toolbar.

3. If necessary, tap the Style button in the resulting popover **A**.

4. Do one or more of the following:

   ▸ Tap to apply one of the six basic photo frame styles.

   ▸ To access more border controls, first tap Style Options, and then in the resulting pane, turn Border to On. Many new controls appear, allowing you to set the border color, width, line style, and 14 additional photo frame styles **B**.

A The style options for photos.

B Turning on the Border control gives you many more options (left). Swipe up to display the additional photo frames (right).

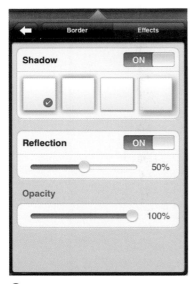

C Use the Effects button to apply drop shadows, reflections, and change the photo's opacity.

▸ To set a drop shadow, reflection effect, or the photo's opacity, first tap Style Options, and then in the resulting pane, tap the Effects button. Turning the Shadow or Reflection options to On displays additional controls for each effect **C**.

Styling Shapes

You have different options when styling shapes than you do when styling photos. You can change the shape's color fill, change its border, apply a drop shadow, and change the shape's opacity.

To style shapes:

1. Select the shape you wish to style.

2. Tap the Info button in the toolbar.

3. If necessary, tap the Style button in the resulting popover .

4. Do one or more of the following:

   ▸ Tap to apply one of the six basic color fills.

   ▸ To access more color fills, tap Style Options, and then, in the resulting pane 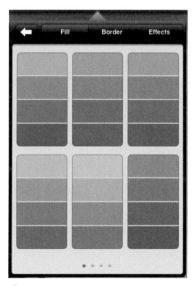, tap the Fill button. You can swipe right or left in this pane for more color options. Tap a color swatch to apply it to the shape.

Ⓐ There are six basic color fills.

Ⓑ Swipe right or left to scroll through the additional color swatches.

C Tap the Border button to change the border color, width, and line style.

D You can add drop shadows to shapes, and change their opacity.

▸ To access border options, tap Style Options, and then, in the resulting pane **C**, tap the Border button. You can change the border color, width, and line style.

▸ To apply effects, tap Style Options, and then, in the resulting pane **D**, tap the Effects button. You can turn on a drop shadow and change the shape's opacity by dragging the slider.

Flipping Graphics

Keynote allows you to flip objects around their horizontal or vertical axes. You use a different technique to flip photos and shapes.

To flip photos:

1. Select the photo you want to flip.
2. Tap the Info button on the toolbar.
3. In the resulting popover, tap the Arrange button **A**.
4. Tap the Flip Vertically or the Flip Horizontally buttons.

   The object flips at your command.

To flip shapes:

1. Select the shape.
2. To flip the shape around its vertical axis, tap either of the two middle selection handles at the sides of the shape, and then drag to the right or left until the object flips over **B**.

   or

   To flip the shape around its horizontal axis, tap either of the two middle selection handles at the top or bottom of the shape, and then drag up or down until the object flips over.

TIP If the shape has text inside, the shape flips its direction, but the text stays in its usual orientation, remaining readable.

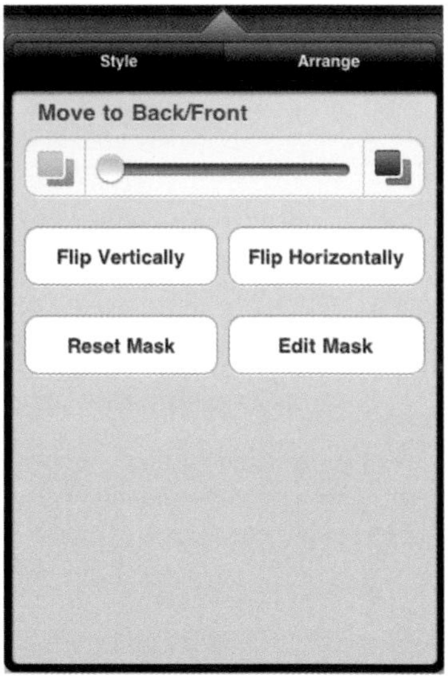

A You can flip photos around their horizontal or vertical axes.

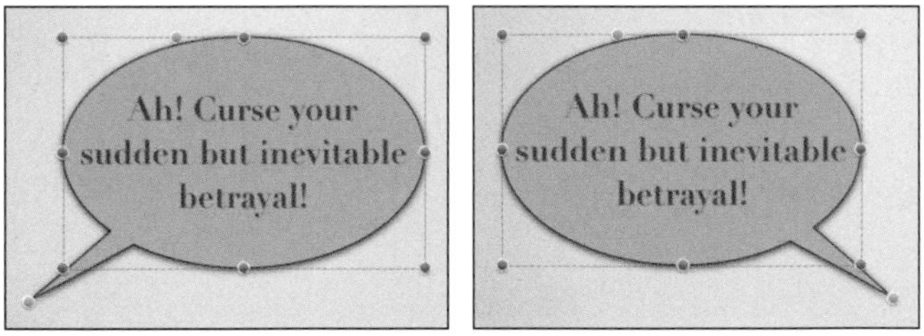

B Flip this shape using its selection handles. After the flip, the quote bubble points in a different direction, but the text is still readable.

 We want the selected photo in front of the other two photos.

Layering Graphics

When you place objects on slides, you can think of each object as being in its own layer on the slide. For example, if you have five objects on a slide, you have six layers: one layer for each object, plus the slide background, which is defined in the slide layout. You can move each of these layers forward and back. The exception is the slide background, the layer furthest back, which can't be brought forward.

Any text boxes that are part of the slide layout, such as the title box and the body box (with or without bulleted text), are part of the background layer, but you can still layer other objects behind these text boxes. Free text boxes that you create on slides can be layered like any other object.

To layer slide objects:

1. Select a slide object that you want to move forward or backward in the slide layers Ⓐ.

2. Tap the Info button in the toolbar, and then tap the Arrange button Ⓑ.

3. Drag the Move to Back/Front slider.

   Dragging the slider to the left moves the object to the bottom of the stack. Dragging it to the right moves the object to the top of the stack.

Ⓑ Use the Move to Back/Front slider to change the position of the object in the layers.

Working with Tables

In presentations, you'll often find it useful to portray data in tables. A table's rows and columns make it easy to present complex information in a simple way. Examples of such data would be quarterly financial results, a performance comparison of two or more products, or sometimes even a simple list.

Keynote provides an excellent set of tools for creating and formatting tables and their contents. These tools allow you to make even dry financial data visually interesting. Using object builds, you can also make parts of your table animate onto the screen, allowing you to build your points one step at a time. You'll find more information about using animation in tables in Chapter 8.

In this chapter, you'll learn how to use Keynote to create and modify a table, and ensure that tables and their content look the way you intend.

Creating a Table

Tables consist of rows and columns. *Rows* are the horizontal divisions of the table; *columns* are the vertical divisions. A row and a column intersect to form a *cell*, which is where you put the contents of a table. You can put text, but not graphics, into a cell.

When you add a table to a slide, Keynote automatically creates a table with five rows and four columns. Of these, the top row is the *header row*, and the left column is the *header column*. A header row or column is formatted differently from the rest of the table to highlight the information in the headers (the exact formatting is specified by the theme designer). You usually put labels in the header row and column, to help people more easily understand your table. Some table layouts include footer rows, which are handy for displaying things like column totals. After the table is added, you can modify the table and its contents by changing the number of rows and columns, formatting the text, modifying table and cell borders, and changing the size of the table.

You're probably familiar with using tables in word processors, such as Microsoft Word or Pages. Using tables in Keynote is similar, with one important caveat: tables in presentations should be simpler than tables that you would use in a printed document. Too much information in a table can overwhelm the audience.

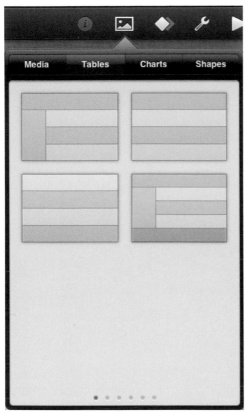

To create a table:

1. In the Slide Navigator, switch to the slide where you want the table.

2. Tap the Media button in the toolbar, and then tap the Tables button in the resulting popover.

   The popover shows four different table layouts **A**. Swiping right or left in the popover shows you different color schemes for these layouts.

3. Tap the layout you want.

   The table appears on the slide **B**.

TIP Because you want to leave enough room on the slide for the table, you'll probably want to choose a slide layout such as Blank or Title & Blank.

TIP If you created a presentation in Keynote '09 and you have images or other graphics within a table, they will be eliminated upon import into Keynote for iPad. Color or gradient fills will be preserved, however.

A Choose the slide layout and color scheme you want for your table.

B Here's our slide with its brand-new table.

Selecting Table Elements

To work effectively with a table, you'll need to know how to select its elements. You can select an entire table, one or more rows and columns, an individual cell, or multiple cells.

Keynote gives you controls to select table elements **Ⓐ**. At the upper-left corner is the *table position handle*, which allows you to drag the whole table around on the slide. The gray bar at the top of the table is the *column selection bar* and the gray bar at the left of the table is the *row selection bar*. The controls at the ends of these selection bars allow you to increase or decrease the number of rows or columns in the table.

Table position handle   Column selection bar   Increase/decrease columns

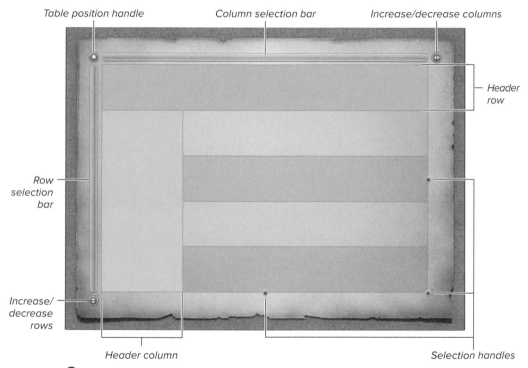

Header row

Row selection bar

Increase/ decrease rows

Header column   Selection handles

Ⓐ In this table, the header row extends across the entire top of the table, and the header column is the light green column on the left.

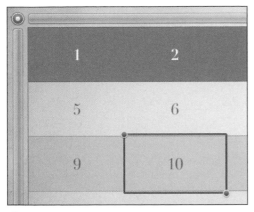

B A selected cell has selection handles at its upper-left and lower-right corners.

C Dragging the cell selection handles extends the selection to additional cells.

To select an entire table:

Tap once anywhere in the table.

Selection handles will appear at the right and bottom edges of the table, which you can use to resize the table **A**.

To select one or more cells:

With no part of the table selected, double-tap in the cell that you wish to select. If any part of the table is selected, tap once on the cell you want.

The border of the selected cell is highlighted in blue, with selection handles at two corners of the cell **B**. You can drag these handles up, down, left, or right to make the selection bigger, covering more cells **C**.

TIP Keynote '09 lets you merge and split table cells, but you can't with Keynote for iPad.

To select an entire row or column:

1. Tap inside a table to select it.

   The row selection bar and the column selection bar appear.

2. To select a row, tap the row selection bar next to the row. The entire row will be outlined in blue **D**.

   or

   To select an entire column, tap the column selection bar above the column. The column will be outlined in blue **E**.

TIP Once you have selected a single row or column, you can use the selection handles to grow the selection to additional rows or columns.

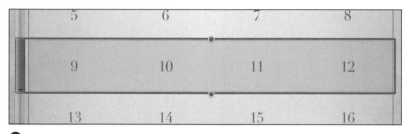

D Use the row selection bar to select an entire row.

E Tap in the column selection bar to select an entire column.

F Tap the up or down buttons to change the number of rows in the table.

G Tap the up or down buttons to change the number of columns in the table.

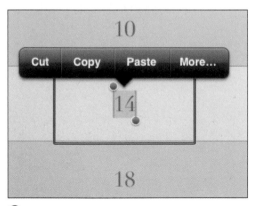

H If there is any text in a cell, double-tapping selects the text. Otherwise, it simply places in insertion point in the cell.

To add or remove rows or columns:

1. Tap inside a table to select it.

2. To change the number of rows in a table, tap the button below the row selection bar **F**.

   or

   To change the number of columns in a table, tap the button to the right of the column selection bar **G**.

3. Tap the up or down arrows in the control you're using to increase or decrease the rows or columns.

TIP Note that increasing the number of rows or columns within a table doesn't change the size of the table; to do that you'll need to use the table's selection handles.

To type in a cell:

Double-tap inside a cell. A text insertion point will start blinking inside the cell; begin typing. If there is already text inside the cell and you double-tap on it, the text will be selected and the Edit popover will appear. Any text you type will replace the text that already appears in the cell **H**.

Working with Table Elements

You can resize tables horizontally or vertically, and also make columns wider and rows taller. If you need to, you can move rows, columns, or even individual cells. When you have table elements you need to delete, you can easily do that, too.

To resize an entire table:

1. Tap anywhere in a table to select it.

   The selection handles will appear at the right and bottom edges of the table.

2. Drag one of the selection handles. To widen the table, drag the handle on the right edge of the table; to make the table taller, drag the handle on the bottom edge of the table; and to make the table grow in both directions simultaneously, drag the handle at the bottom-right corner of the table.

To resize rows or columns:

1. Tap inside a table to select it.

   The row selection bar and the column selection bar appear.

2. Select a row by tapping the row selection bar next to the row. The entire row will be outlined in blue.

   or

   Select a column by tapping the column selection bar above the column. The column will be outlined in blue.

3. To resize the row, drag the handle at the bottom edge of the blue bar at the left edge of the row Ⓐ.

   or

   To resize the column, drag the handle at the right edge of the blue bar at the top of the column Ⓐ.

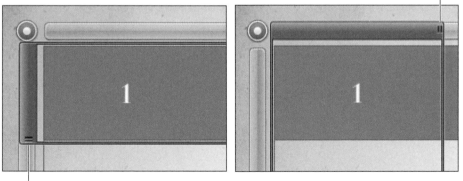

Column resize handle

Row resize handle

Ⓐ Drag the row or column resize handles to change those element's size.

To move rows or columns:

1. Tap inside a table to select it.

   The row selection bar and the column selection bar appear.

2. Tap the row or column selection bar.

   The row or column highlights.

3. Touch and hold the blue part of the selection bar next to the selected row or column, and then drag it to the new position in the table **B**.

TIP By default, most Keynote table styles have alternating row colors turned on. When you move a row, the moved row preserves the color alternation.

To move cells:

1. Slow double-tap a cell to select it.

2. Touch and hold the cell, and then drag it to the new position **C**.

   The moved cell replaces the contents (if any) of the destination cell, and leaves a blank cell behind.

To delete elements:

1. Slow double-tap to select the element, whether it's a row, column, or a cell with content. To select an entire table, slow double-tap the table position handle.

   The Edit popover appears.

2. Tap Delete.

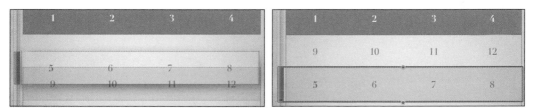

B Drag the blue bar in the row or column selection bar to move the element (left) to its destination (right).

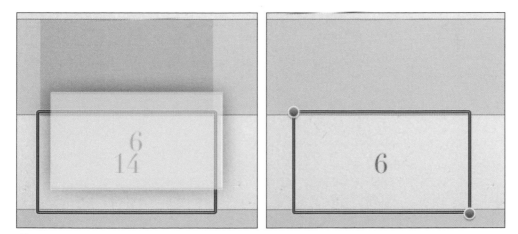

C While you're moving a cell you see a ghost image of it (left) and when the move is complete the original cell is empty (right).

Formatting and Styling Tables

Once you have the layout of your table set to your liking, you can begin working on the table's look, including the formatting of the text within the table. One limitation in Keynote is that all the text in a table must be the same font and font size. But you can style text in other ways.

If you want to apply alignment to the contents of a single cell, or group of cells, you must select the cell or cells first, and there are separate controls for horizontal and vertical alignment.

To set table formatting options:

1. Tap inside a table to select it.

2. Tap the Info button in the toolbar. If the Table pane isn't visible in the resulting popover, tap the Tables button.

3. Tap Table Options. The Table Options pane appears .

4. Do one or more of the following:

   ▸ Turn the Table Border off (it is on by default).

   ▸ Turn Alternating Rows off (they are on by default). This refers to alternating light and dark row colors.

   ▸ Tap Grid Options to display the different table line options 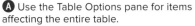. Then turn the different options on or off.

   ▸ Change the Text Size or Table Font. The choices in Text Size are Tiny, Small, Medium, Large, and Extra Large. The Table Font choices include all the fonts on your iPad.

🅐 Use the Table Options pane for items affecting the entire table.

🅑 You can turn lines in the table on or off using Grid Options.

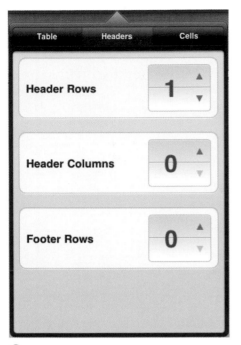

C Change the number of header rows, header columns, or footer rows.

To change the number of header rows or columns:

1. Tap inside a table to select it.

2. Tap the Info button in the toolbar. If the Headers pane isn't visible in the resulting popover, tap the Headers button. The Headers pane appears **C**.

3. Tap the up or down arrows to change the number of Header Rows, Header Columns, or Footer Rows.

Saving Tables for Later Use

It can take a considerable amount of effort to format a table that's just the way you want, and there's no reason you can't reuse that same formatted table again and again. For this and other reasons, it's a good idea to create a Keynote library file that you can use to store objects you want to save for later.

To build a library file, create a new Keynote presentation using one of the neutral themes such as White or Gradient, with one or more slides based on the Blank slide layout. Use the My Presentations view to switch to your existing presentation file and copy an object you want to save. Switch back to the library file and paste the object in. Repeat as necessary for any elements you think you'll want to reuse.

To change the formatting of text in cells:

1. Slow double-tap a cell to select it.

2. (Optional) Drag the selection handle to extend the selection to multiple cells.

3. Tap the Info button in the toolbar. If the Cells pane isn't visible in the resulting popover, tap the Cells button. The Cells pane appears **D**.

   Most of the options in this pane are the same as the text formatting options anywhere else in Keynote. Refer to Chapter 4 for information on the text styling, text color, and alignment controls. The Fill Color option leads you to a color picker that can change the background color of the selected cells. The Border Style option leads you to a pane with different border options **E**. Finally, the Wrap Text in Cell option, which is on by default, allows you to make text stretch across multiple cell boundaries.

D Style the text within tables in the Cells pane.

E Use the Border Style pane to turn on or off borders for individual cells.

7

Creating Charts

Charts can help viewers of your presentation better understand quantitative information without overwhelming them with an avalanche of numbers. Using a chart, you can present complex data that can be understood at a glance. Charts illustrate the relationships between different sets of data, and they are also good for showing trends over time.

Keynote provides you with a wide variety of chart types, and you can manipulate those charts in many different ways to get your point across. You should have no problems tailoring your charts to suit your taste and the needs of your presentation.

You can also animate the parts of a chart to have them appear on your slide one at a time. To create these chart builds, see Chapter 8.

In this chapter, you'll learn about the different chart types; how to use Keynote to create charts; and how to manipulate those charts so that they look the way you want.

In This Chapter

About Chart Types

Keynote can create nine different types of charts, as shown in **Table 7.1**. Each type of chart is useful for displaying particular kinds of data.

It's not always easy to decide on which kind of chart to use. Sometimes the data that you're trying to present will practically beg for a particular chart type; for example, when you're trying to show values as percentages that add up to 100%, a pie chart is almost always the right approach. But in other instances, several chart types might fit your data and do a good job of presenting it. Here are a few tips to help you choose the right chart for the job.

- Evaluate the data that you are trying to present, particularly the aspect of the data that you want to highlight. Data

where the totals are more important than the individual values are good candidates for area charts, stacked bar charts, and stacked column charts.

- If you have many data series to present, use a chart type like bar or column, which show many data points well.

- Choose the chart type that produces the simplest chart for your data. If necessary, switch between the different types in Keynote to see the visual effect of each type on the data. Because your viewers don't have control of how long your slide is on screen, it helps to give them charts they can grasp quickly.

- Pie charts shouldn't be used to represent data with more than 5 to 8 data series. Each series will appear as a slice of the pie, and too-small pieces will not have good visual impact.

TABLE 7.1 Chart Types

Icon	Chart Type	Description
	Column Chart	Column charts show unique values. They are useful when comparing values, such as sales, over different time periods.
	Stacked Column Chart	Stacked column charts, like area charts, display both individual values and the sum of several values for a given item.
	Bar Chart	Bar charts, like column charts, show individual items and their relationship to one another.
	Stacked Bar Chart	This variation of the bar chart is similar to the stacked column chart.
	Area Chart	Area charts show the magnitude of change over time.
	Stacked Area Chart	Stacked area charts show the magnitude of change over time, and they display both individual values and the sum of all values in the chart.
	Line Chart	Line charts show data trends over time or other intervals. They are useful for showing variations in values, such as stock prices.
	Pie Chart	Pie charts show proportional relationships between several values and a whole, often expressed as percentages.
	Scatter Chart	Scatter charts show the relationship between two or more sets of variables. Often used for scientific, statistical, and engineering data.

Chart anatomy

Before you begin creating charts, you'll need to know a little about the terminology Keynote uses to refer to the different parts of a chart, and the different tools that Keynote gives you to manipulate charts. The column chart shown in **A** labels the main parts that appear on a slide. When you double-tap a chart, it spins around and Keynote provides the Chart Data Editor, which is a spreadsheet-like view where you enter the information that makes up the chart **B**. As usual, you'll be able to customize the chart with tools available from the Info button in the toolbar.

continues on next page

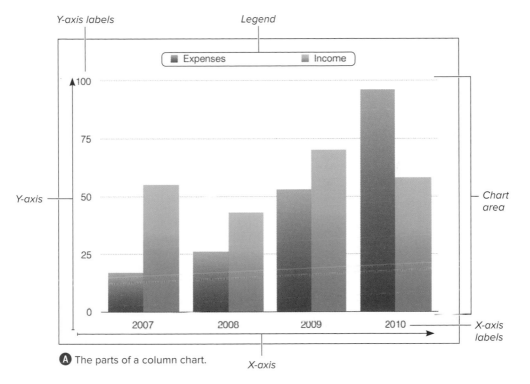

A The parts of a column chart.

B The Chart Data Editor resembles a spreadsheet, but it doesn't do any calculations.

The data for the chart appear in the *chart area*, which contains the bars, columns, lines, etc. All chart types (except for pie charts) have two axes, the horizontal *X-axis* and the vertical *Y-axis*. One of these will be the *value axis*, which is where you read the values you are charting. For example, in Ⓐ, the value axis is the Y-axis. In column charts, area charts, and line charts, the Y-axis is the value axis. For bar charts, the X-axis is the value axis. Pie charts don't have a value axis.

Charts show the relationship between two types of data (for example, financial performance over a time period such as months or years). These two data types are called the *data series* and *data sets*. In Ⓑ, each row in the Chart Data Editor represents a data series, and each column represents a data set. The *legend* is the label or labels on the chart that explain what the different data series represent.

Charting Alternatives

Keynote's charting abilities are decent, but they are hardly complete. For example, Keynote doesn't provide 3-D charts, and lacks many chart types found in other charting programs. Keynote also lacks the ability to create combination charts, which contain more than one chart type. If you need more charting power than Keynote can provide, you'll need to turn to other applications that can create charts.

On the iPad, a good alternative for creating graphs on the fly is the Omni Group's OmniGraphSketcher. This program lets you easily draw graphs on your iPad Ⓒ. You can export graphs made in the program to your Photos library to access them in Keynote, or you can simply copy and paste between the two programs.

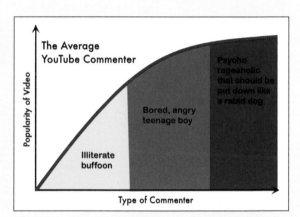

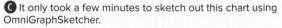

Ⓒ It only took a few minutes to sketch out this chart using OmniGraphSketcher.

On the Mac, Microsoft Excel has many chart types that Keynote lacks, including 3-D, surface, stock, radar, bubble, and doughnut charts. Excel gives you control over the transparency of chart objects, which allows you to create some nice effects. Because Excel's charting abilities are coupled with a powerful spreadsheet, you can do all of your calculations in Excel, chart your results, dress up the chart using Excel's advanced tools, and then save the finished chart as an image that you can move from the Mac into the iPad's Photo library and then into Keynote.

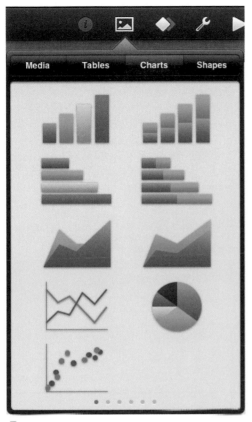

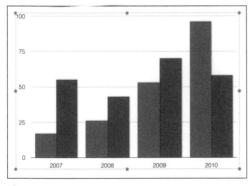

A Use the Charts pane of the Media popover to choose one of the nine chart types.

B This simple chart appears whenever you add a chart to a slide.

Adding Charts

You'll want to add a chart to a slide that has plenty of room for the chart, though you can add a chart to any slide. Of the built-in slide layouts, the one that is most appropriate for charts is Blank, which should be your go-to layout to use for charts that need to be as large as possible. Title & Blank is also a good choice, and the title on this layout is already well-matched to the rest of your presentation.

To add a chart to a slide:

1. Display the slide where you want to add a chart.

2. Tap the Media button in the toolbar and then tap the Charts button **A**.

   The Charts pane of the Media popover appears. You can swipe right or left to see the nine different types of charts in different color schemes.

3. Tap the chart type that you want.

   A chart of the type you selected, using sample data, appears on the slide **B**.

4. Double-tap on the chart to enter data into the Chart Data Editor.

   For more information about using the Chart Data Editor, see the next section.

TIP You can add as many charts as you want to a slide, subject only to how many will fit on the slide, and to your sense of good taste.

Editing Chart Data

When you create a new chart in Keynote, the Chart Data Editor is filled by default with two rows and four columns of sample data. First, you'll need to change the row and column labels so that they match your data. After that, you can enter your data in the Chart Data Editor's cells.

Once your data is in place, it can be rearranged by dragging rows or columns around.

To enter your own chart data:

1. Double-tap on the chart with the sample data.

   The chart spins around and displays the Chart Data Editor 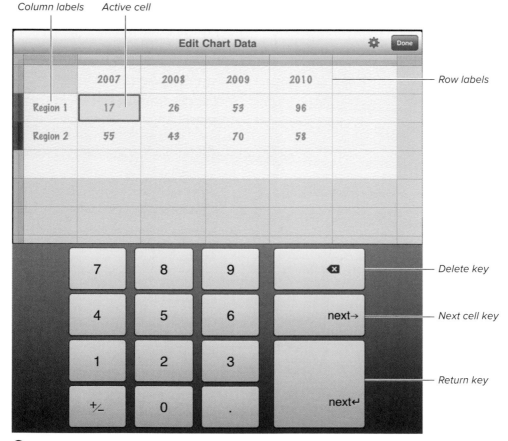. You begin in the upper-left cell of the Editor's data area. Because you're in a cell that only accepts numeric values, the on-screen numeric keypad appears.

Column labels   Active cell

Row labels

Delete key

Next cell key

Return key

Ⓐ Enter your chart's data, replacing the sample data in the Chart Data Editor. Because we're entering numeric data, the on-screen number pad appears.

2. Double-tap the name of the row or column that you want to change.

Because you're now in a cell that accepts alphanumeric entries, the on-screen keyboard appears (unless you're using an external keyboard), and the cell is highlighted.

3. Type the new name.

4. Tap the next label you want to change, and type in the new name. Repeat this for the rest of the row and column labels.

5. Tap the first data cell to highlight it.

The on-screen numeric keypad reappears.

6. Type a value into each of the cells **B**.

7. Tap Done.

The chart spins into view with your new labels and data **C**.

TIP When you're using the Apple Wireless Keyboard, the right and left arrow keys work to move around in the Chart Data Editor, but the up and down arrow keys don't. The Tab key works, as does the Return key. The Tab, Return, and right arrow keys also add rows or columns to the spreadsheet if you get to the end of the current cells.

Edit Chart Data				⚙ Done
	2007	2008	2009	2010
North Bay	33	33	29	54
San Francisco	44	42	49	48
East Bay	38	34	33	37

B When you're finished entering data, tap the Done button.

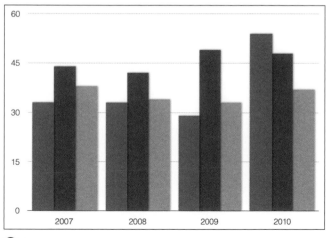

C The new chart now reflects the data you entered.

To move rows or columns:

In the Chart Data Editor, touch, hold, and drag the bar adjacent to one of the row or column labels **D**.

To edit entire rows or columns:

1. In the Chart Data Editor, tap the bar adjacent to one of the row or column labels **D**.

2. Tap Insert, Cut, Copy, Paste, or Delete.

	Insert	Cut	Copy	Paste	Delete
	2007		**2008**		**2009**
North Bay	33		33		29
San Francisco	44		42		49
East Bay	38		34		33

D You can move rows or columns by dragging the blue bar next to the element you're moving.

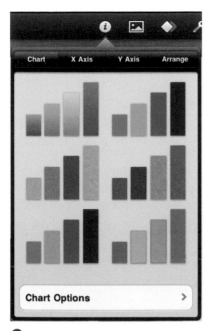

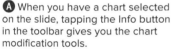

A When you have a chart selected on the slide, tapping the Info button in the toolbar gives you the chart modification tools.

Changing Chart Types

You can change the chart type at any time in Keynote. All you need to do is select the chart and then choose a new type from the Info popover.

To change the chart type:

1. Select a chart on the Slide Canvas.

2. Tap the Info button in the toolbar.

   The Chart popover appears **A**.

3. At the bottom of the popover, tap Chart Options.

   The Chart Options pane appears **B**.

4. Tap Chart Type and then choose the new kind of chart you want in the resulting Chart Type pane **C**.

Chart Options	
Chart Title	OFF
Legend	OFF
Border	OFF
Text Size	Medium >
Chart Font	Default >
Value Labels	Off >
Chart Type	Column >

B One of the things you can do in the Chart Options pane is change the chart type.

C Pick the new chart type from the list.

Transposing Chart Plots

Sometimes you need to look at your data in a different way, and Keynote can transpose the way it plots the data series and data sets, to give you a different perspective.

In **A**, the rows (data series) in the Chart Data Editor show income and expense figures distributed across four months, which are expressed in the columns (data sets). The resulting graph **B** groups each month's financial results together. If we transpose the data series and data sets, we get a very different view of the same data **C**. In this view, you can see how income and expenses change over the four months. The income figures and the expense figures for all months are grouped together, making it easier to see the trend for each group over time. Keynote changes the legend of the graph to reflect the new ordering of the data, and the labels in the Chart Data Editor also change to match.

The benefit of being able to transpose data series and data sets is that it allows you to change the presentation of the data in the Chart Data Editor without the need to retype your data.

A The rows in the Chart Data Editor represent the data series.

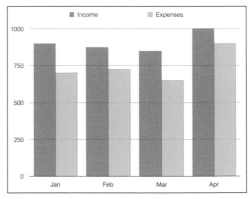

B When charted, the data series group the financial data together by month.

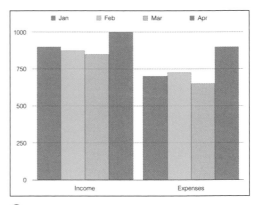

C By transposing the data series and data sets, you see all the income and all the expense figures grouped together.

To transpose data series and data sets:

1. Double-tap a chart on a slide.

   The Chart Data Editor appears.

2. Tap the Settings button and then choose the unchecked setting in the resulting popover **D**.

   The chart changes.

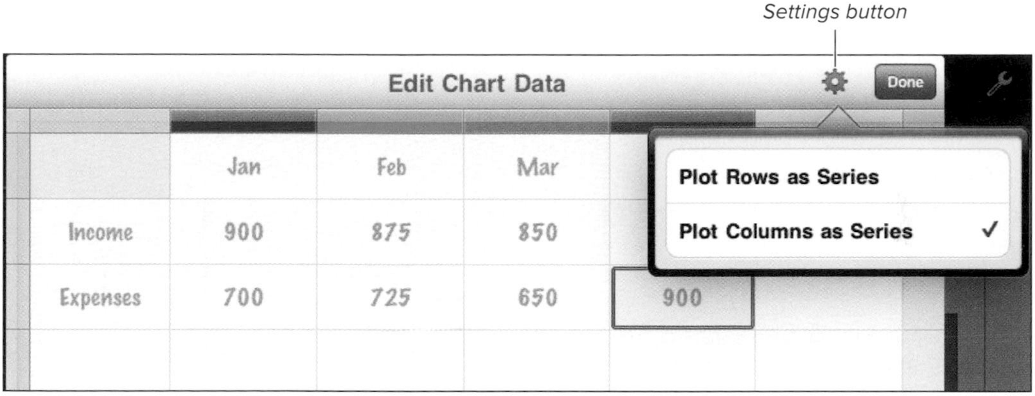

Settings button

	Jan	Feb	Mar	
Income	900	875	850	
Expenses	700	725	650	900

Edit Chart Data ⚙ Done

Plot Rows as Series

Plot Columns as Series ✓

D Use the Settings button in the Chart Data Editor to transpose data sets.

Modifying Chart Elements

You can format the different parts of a chart to serve your needs. You can change elements that affect the whole chart, or just elements that affect the X-axis or the Y-axis.

To change chart options:

1. Select a chart on the Slide Canvas.
2. Tap the Info button in the toolbar.

   The Chart popover appears.
3. At the bottom of the Chart pane of the popover, tap Chart Options.

   The Chart Options pane appears **A**.

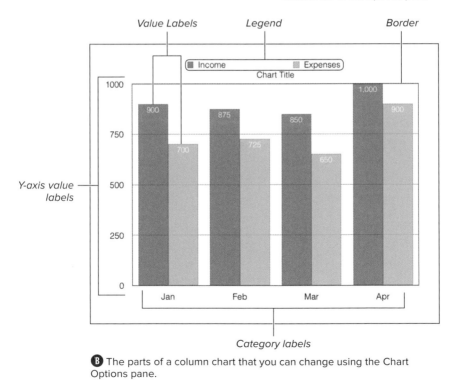

A You can customize many aspects of the chart in the Chart Options pane.

B The parts of a column chart that you can change using the Chart Options pane.

Chart	X Axis	Y Axis	Arrange

Category Labels ON

Series Names OFF

Label Angle >

Major Gridlines OFF

Major Tick Marks OFF

Title OFF

Axis Line ON

C Change X-axis options using this pane.

4. Do one or more of the following **B**:

  ▸ Turn on Chart Title, Legend, or Border.

  ▸ Change the Text Size. Your choices are Tiny, Small, Medium (shown), Large, and Extra Large.

  ▸ Change the Chart Font. You may choose from any of the fonts available on the iPad. The Default choice shown in **A** denotes the font chosen by the presentation theme designer; there's not really a font called "Default."

  ▸ Turn on Value Labels. These are labels that appear within or outside the graphics in column or bar charts, and show you the numeric value that graphic represents.

TIP Keynote can only use one font and one text size for items that you can change in the chart.

TIP You can use a Chart Title if the chart needs, well, a title, but I'm not a big fan of it. It must use the same font and size as the rest of the chart. You'll get more flexibility by using the Title & Blank slide layout, or even a free text box.

To change X-axis elements:

1. Select a chart on the Slide Canvas.

2. Tap the Info button in the toolbar.

   The Chart popover appears.

3. Tap the X Axis button **C**.

continues on next page

4. Do one or more of the following:

- Turn off Category Labels (they are on by default) **B**.

- Turn on Series Names. This is most useful when you have transposed plots (see above). You can then show both the category and series names to make your chart more understandable, without resorting to chart legends **D**.

- Set the Label Angle. This is set to Horizontal by default, but your other choices are Left Vertical, Left Diagonal, Right Diagonal, and Right Vertical.

- Turn on Major Gridlines or Major Tick Marks.

- Turn on the X Axis Title. This is an additional title that appears below the X-axis. It appears with the placeholder text *Category Axis*, which you can change.

- Turn off the Axis Line (on by default). This is a line that appears at the bottom of the chart and delineates the X-axis.

TIP Column and Stacked Column charts usually look better without gridlines in the X-axis, and with gridlines turned on in the Y-axis. The reverse is true for Bar and Stacked Bar charts. Line charts often look good with gridlines turned on for both axes.

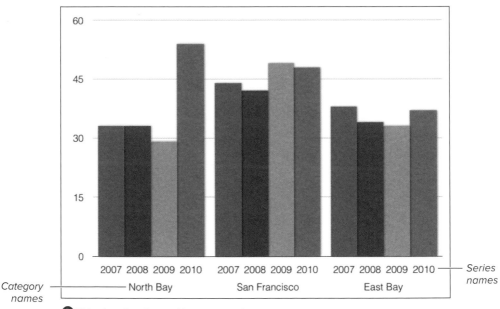

D This chart has Series Names turned on.

E Change Y-axis options using this pane.

F You can change the way numbers in the Y-axis are displayed using this pane.

To change Y-axis elements:

1. Select a chart on the Slide Canvas.

2. Tap the Info button in the toolbar.

   The Chart popover appears.

3. Tap the Y Axis button **E**.

4. Do one or more of the following (swipe to scroll the pane and show the last two items in this list):

   ▸ Turn off Value Labels which are on by default (shown as Y-axis value labels **B**).

   ▸ Tap Number Format to get to the Number Format pane **F**. In this pane, you can set the decimals in the Y-axis labels, turn on comma or period separators, type a prefix or suffix for the labels, and format how negative numbers are shown.

   ▸ Change the Label Angle. You have the same options as with the X Axis Label Angles.

   continues on next page

- ▸ Tap to change the Value Scale Settings **G**.

- ▸ Set Major Gridlines (on by default), Minor Gridlines, Major Tick Marks, or Minor Tick Marks (all off by default).

- ▸ Turn on the Y Axis Title. This is an additional title that appears next to the Y-axis. It appears with the place-holder text *Value Axis*, which you can change.

- ▸ Turn off the Axis Line (on by default). This is a line that appears at the left of the chart and delineates the Y-axis.

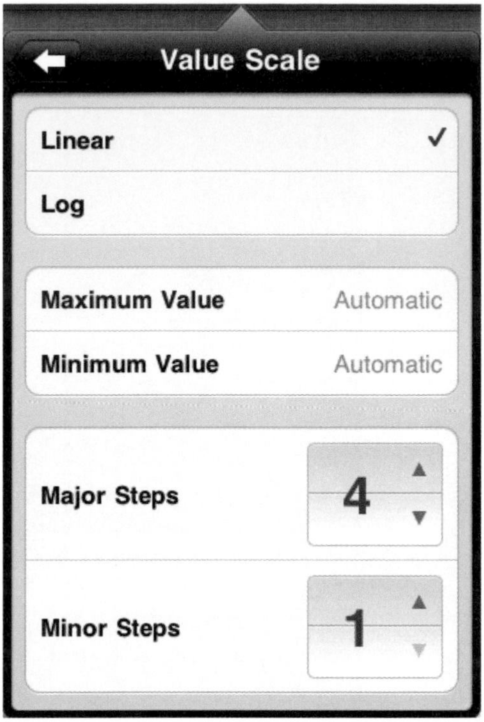

G Modify the scales shown for items in the values axis, or Y-axis.

Working with Pie Charts

Pie charts work a bit differently than the other charts in Keynote. Because a pie chart doesn't have an X-axis or Y-axis, Keynote charts only the first data set in the Chart Data Editor. If the data series are in rows in the Chart Data Editor, only the first column will be charted. If the data series are in columns in the Chart Data Editor, only the first row will be charted. A single pie chart represents a single data set, and each wedge in the pie chart represents one element of that set. If there are other data sets in the Chart Data Editor, and you switch the chart type to a pie chart, the excess data sets won't disappear, but they won't be used, either.

Because pie charts are different, the Info popover changes to reflect those differences. For example, because a pie chart does not have more than one axis, the only panes that appear are Chart and Arrange.

Keynote allows you to manipulate the individual wedges of a pie chart separately. You can select a wedge and manually drag it away ("explode it") from the main body of the pie chart for effect.

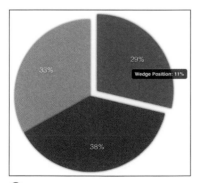

A You can explode one or more wedges from a pie chart by dragging the wedges.

To explode a pie chart:

1. Select the chart.
2. Touch and hold to select a single wedge and drag to explode it from the rest of the chart **A**.

   As you move the wedge, a popover shows how far, in percentage units, you've moved the wedge from the rest of the chart.

To set pie chart options:

1. Select the chart.
2. Tap the Info button in the toolbar.

   The Chart popover appears **B**.

continues on next page

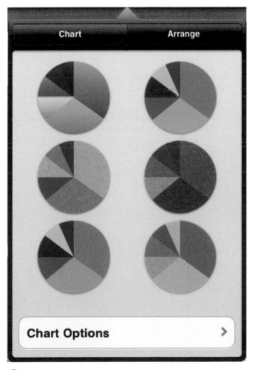

B Choose from pie chart color schemes in the Chart pane of the Info popover when you have a pie chart selected.

3. Tap the Chart button .

4. At the bottom of the Chart pane of the popover, tap Chart Options.

   The Chart Options pane appears 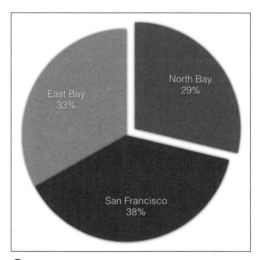C.

5. Do one or more of the following:

   ▸ Turn on Chart Title or Legend.

   ▸ Change the Text Size. Your choices are Tiny, Small, Medium, Large, and Extra Large.

   ▸ Change the Chart Font. You may choose from any of the fonts available on the iPad.

   ▸ Turn on Value Labels. These are labels that appear inside or outside pie wedges, and show you the numeric value that graphic represents. In the pane you see when you tap Value Labels, you can also turn on Series Name, which displays them with the value labels D.

   ▸ Set the way numbers are displayed in the pie with the Number Format option. The options here are similar to those shown in figure F of "Modifying Chart Elements."

Chart Options

| Chart Title | OFF |
| Legend | OFF |

| Text Size | Medium > |
| Chart Font | Default > |

| Value Labels | Inside > |
| Number Format | > |

| Chart Type | Pie > |

C Pie chart options are slightly different than those of other chart types.

East Bay 33%

North Bay 29%

San Francisco 38%

D With a pie chart, it's especially useful to display series names and values together.

Using Transitions and Animations

Once you have created all the elements of your presentation, you can add motion and visual appeal to your slideshow with slide transitions and animations.

Slide transitions are animated effects that occur when you switch from one slide to another. An *object build* is an animation that occurs within the body of the slide. Some builds involve one or more elements of an object, and you can control how objects arrive on a slide and how they leave. For example, you can have the parts of a graph appear on the screen one at a time (called a *chart build*), or make text boxes or graphics fly on or off the screen. *Text builds* animate the way different lines of bulleted text appear on the slide. *Table builds* let you animate parts of a table onto the screen.

In this chapter, you'll learn how to apply slide transitions and create the different types of object builds.

In This Chapter

Applying Slide Transitions

Slide transitions are a good way to add visual interest when you change slides. They also serve as a cue for the audience to reinforce the fact that you're changing slides; if someone isn't paying particularly close attention, that flash of motion will often help them refocus on your slideshow.

All slide transitions involve an animated effect where the first, old slide is replaced by the second, new slide. Keynote provides 21 built-in transition styles, plus None.

You apply transitions using the Slide Navigator and the Transitions and Animations button in the toolbar. You can set a transition between any two contiguous slides. Many transitions have options that you can set to adjust the look of the effect. For example, you can set a page flip transition to move from left to right, right to left, top to bottom, or bottom to top. You can also control (to a point) the speed of a transition.

To apply a slide transition:

1. In the Slide Navigator, tap to select the slide you want to apply the transition to.

2. Tap the Transitions and Animation button in the toolbar Ⓐ.

   Keynote switches to the Transitions and Animation mode, and a button appears next to the slide you selected, showing you the transition assigned to that slide. If no transition has been assigned, the button reads None Ⓑ.

Transitions and Animations

Ⓐ Start applying a slide transition by tapping the Transitions and Animations button in the toolbar.

Transition button   Preview

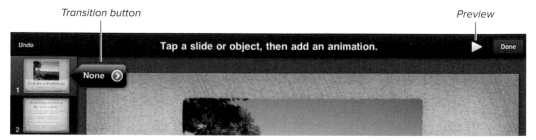

Ⓑ When you're in Transitions and Animations mode, a button shows in the Slide Navigator telling you what, if any, transition is applied to the selected slide.

C Use the Transitions popover to set the transition effect you want.

Transition indicator   *Preview button*

D In Transitions and Animations mode, a yellow triangle on a slide thumbnail indicates that you've applied a transition. To repeat the transition, tap the Preview button in the popover.

3. Tap the transitions button.

The Transitions popover appears **C**.

4. Swipe up or down until you find the transition you want, and then tap it.

The popover disappears for a moment, Keynote shows a preview of the transition, and then the popover reappears. To see the preview again, tap the Preview button at the top right corner of the Transitions popover **D**.

5. Tap on the slide to make the Transitions popover disappear.

Slides with transitions appear in the Slide Navigator (when you're in the Transitions and Animation mode) with a small yellow triangle in the lower-right corner, as in **D**.

6. If you want to add more transitions, repeat the preceding steps. To preview the transition, tap the Preview button in the toolbar. To finish and leave the Transitions and Animation mode, tap Done in the upper right corner of the screen.

> **TIP** You can't apply a transition to more than one slide in the Slide Navigator at a time. This is such an incredible drawback that I assume that a later version of Keynote will fix it, perhaps by the time you read this. In the meantime, here's a workaround: you can apply a transition to a particular slide and then duplicate it as many times as you need. Of course, if you change slide layouts, you'll have to apply the transition again.

> **TIP** You can use slide transitions to communicate different types of information or to denote sections in your presentation. For example, you can use a transition to signify that you're moving to an entirely different topic in your presentation. Let's say that you have a presentation with three distinct sections. You can use no transitions between the slides in each section, and use transitions only between slides at the end of one section and the beginning of the next.

To set a transition's options:

1. While the Transitions popover is open, tap the Option button. The options for the currently applied transition appear ⓔ. Different transitions have different options (for example, the transition shown in ⓔ has a direction control), so these options will change. All transitions, however, share a set of options:

   ▸ **Duration** has a slider that allows you to change the length of the transition from the default one second to five seconds, in quarter-second increments.

   ▸ **Start Transition** has two values. On Tap requires a tap on the screen to trigger the transition, and After Previous Transition proceeds with the transition automatically.

   ▸ **Delay** is a slider that becomes active only when you choose After Previous Transition. It has a half-second default value, and can be increased up to 10 seconds.

2. When you're done setting the transition's options, tap elsewhere on the slide. To finish and leave the Transitions and Animation mode, tap Done in the upper right corner of the screen.

ⓔ The Options pane of the Transitions popover allows you to set a variety of options, such as the transition direction.

Less Really Is More

When it comes to slide transitions, restraint really should be the order of the day. Chances are you've seen presentations where presenters used way too many transitions and animated effects. Did you like them? No? That's what I thought.

Too-busy slide transitions and animations of objects on the slide can easily distract the audience from the content of your presentation. Make sure not to overdo them, or you might find your audience slipping out of the room before your talk is over. Too much swooping and spinning can even make some audience members nauseous!

A Keynote begins the Magic Move by asking if you want to duplicate the current slide.

B Each of the objects (in this case three different text boxes) shows a star icon, indicating that it is part of a Magic Move.

Creating Magic Moves

A *Magic Move* is a kind of transition that takes one or more common objects from one slide and animates changes to those objects in different sizes, positions, or effects on the next slide. For example, if you have the same image in different positions on adjacent slides, applying a Magic Move transition creates the animation effect of the image moving from its original position to its new position on the second slide.

Begin by preparing a slide with objects you want to move. As part of the transition, you'll duplicate the slide and then apply the Magic Move transition. Then you can resize, move, or add effects to objects on the original or duplicated slide. When you play the presentation, Keynote creates the required animation.

To create a Magic Move:

1. In the Slide Navigator, tap to select the slide you want to use for the Magic Move.

2. Tap the Transitions and Animation button in the toolbar.

   Keynote switches to the Transitions and Animation mode, and the transitions button appears next to the selected slide.

3. Tap the transitions button and then tap Magic Move from the Transitions popover.

   Keynote asks you if you want to duplicate the slide A.

4. Tap Yes.

   Keynote creates the duplicated slide, and switches you to it. Each of the objects on the slide is marked with a star icon, to indicate that it is part of a Magic Move B.

continues on next page

5. Arrange the objects on the duplicated slide however you'd like them to appear **C**.

6. To see the Magic Move in action, tap the Preview button in the toolbar. To finish and leave the Transitions and Animation mode, tap Done in the upper right corner of the screen.

TIP You can start objects off the screen by pinching in the Slide Canvas to zoom out to 50% view and then move the objects off the slide and onto the Slide Canvas **D**. When the Magic Move occurs, the objects rush onto the slide.

C During the Magic Move, the text boxes moved into place, and the three pictures flew in from off the slide.

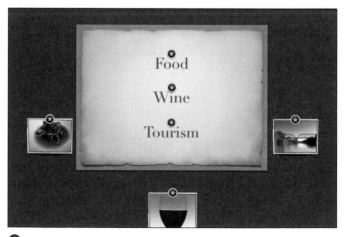

D In this 50% view, you can see how the pictures were positioned off the slide area on the original slide.

A I haven't applied any builds yet, so the Build In and Build Out buttons show None.

B Choose the build effect you want from the popover.

Animating Bulleted Text

Object builds, as noted earlier, animate one or more objects on the slide. When you create a build, you can set the way the object "builds in" (appears on the slide) and "builds out" (leaves the slide).

Probably the most common sort of build you will be doing is with bulleted text, to make each bullet and its associated text appear when you tap the iPad during the presentation. These text builds have a number of options so that you can control how the text appears on the slide. If you want to animate free text boxes, see "Creating Object Builds" later in this chapter.

To apply bulleted text builds:

1. Switch to a slide with bulleted text.

2. Tap the Transitions and Animation button in the toolbar.

   Keynote switches to the Transitions and Animation mode.

3. Tap to select the box containing the bulleted text.

   Buttons appear next to the object, showing any build effect that's already been applied to it. Of course, if the text has no build the Build In and Build Out buttons show None **A**.

4. Tap either the Build In or Build Out button.

   A popover appears showing the available effects **B**.

continues on next page

5. Tap the effect that you want.

   Keynote shows you a preview of the effect.

6. (Optional) Tap the Options button at the bottom of the popover to adjust the build duration, when the build should start, and the delay (if the build begins automatically).

7. (Optional) Tap the Delivery button at the bottom of the popover to adjust how the build delivers the effect (for bulleted text, typically all at once or one bullet point at a time) **C**.

8. (Optional) Tap the Order button to control the order of multiple object builds. See "Ordering Object Builds" later in this chapter for more information.

C The Delivery pane changes, depending on what sort of object you are building. This is the Delivery pane for a bulleted text box.

Animating Charts and Tables

You can animate Keynote tables and charts so that the parts of the element appear on the screen in sequence. This adds some visual flair to the item, and can even add a touch of drama. Chart builds rank just behind bulleted text builds in usefulness. You can get some dramatic effects when you make the parts of a chart appear sequentially on the screen.

To add a build to a table or chart:

1. Switch to a slide with the table or chart you want to animate.

2. Tap the Transitions and Animation button in the toolbar.

   Keynote switches to the Transitions and Animation mode.

3. Tap to select the table or chart.

   Buttons appear next to the object, showing any build effect that's already been applied to it. If the text has no build, the Build In and Build Out buttons show None.

4. Tap either the Build In or Build Out button.

   A popover appears showing the available effects **A**.

5. Tap the effect that you want.

   Keynote shows you a preview of the effect.

6. (Optional) Tap the Options button at the bottom of the popover to adjust the build duration, when the build should start, and the delay (if the build begins automatically).

7. (Optional) Tap the Delivery button at the bottom of the popover to adjust how the build delivers the effect **B**.

continues on next page

A Choose the build effect you want.

B The Delivery pane for chart objects.

Tables and charts have different delivery options, as described in **Table 8.1** and **Table 8.2**, respectively.

8. (Optional) Tap the Order button to control the order of multiple object builds. See "Ordering Object Builds" later in this chapter for more information.

TABLE 8.1 Table Delivery Options

Option	What It Does
All at Once	Builds the entire contents of the table onto or off of the slide.
By Row	Builds each row of the table onto or off of the slide, one at a time. The rows begin with the top of the table and work down.
By Column	Builds each column of the table onto or off of the slide, one at a time. The columns begin with the leftmost column of the table and work to the right.
By Cell	Brings each cell onto or off of the slide, one at a time. The cells begin with the upper-leftmost cells, and work across, and then down.
By Row Content	First brings on the table background (the grid) and then causes the contents of the table to appear, one row at a time.
By Column Content	First brings on the table background (the grid) and then causes the contents of the table to appear, one column at a time.
By Cell Content	First brings on the table background (the grid) and then causes the contents of the table to appear, one cell at a time.

There are also Reverse options for each of the options above; these reverse the direction of the delivery.

TABLE 8.2 Chart Delivery Options

Option	What It Does
All at Once	Builds the entire contents of the chart onto or off of the slide.
Background First	Builds the chart background first, followed by the other elements of the chart (bars, columns, or area shapes).
By Series	Builds each data series onto or off of the slide, one at a time.
By Set	Builds each data set onto the chart, one at a time.
By Element in Series	Builds each element in a data series, one at a time.
By Element in Set	Builds each element in a data set, one at a time.

Creating Object Builds

General object builds work much the same way as the previous builds in this chapter. The only difference is that you will be working with any element that you can place on the Slide Canvas, including text boxes, shapes, graphics, or movies. Actually, to Keynote, everything on the Slide Canvas is an object, including bulleted text boxes, tables, and charts, so you can animate almost everything.

When you are animating multiple objects, you can control the order in which those objects appear, and each object can have its own build style, direction, and delivery options. So you can, for example, have a slide with bulleted text that moves in from the left side, a graphic that slides in on the right side, and a title box that drops in from the top . You can set the order in which objects appear on the screen, and for each object, you can choose to have it appear after you tap the slide, with the prior object, or after the prior object.

Ⓐ This slide has multiple object builds. The title box animates in from the top of the slide, and the bulleted text box and the picture move in from the left and right side of the slide, respectively. Yes, that would be tasteless in a real presentation; it's only an example.

To animate several objects:

1. Switch to a slide you want to animate.

2. Tap the Transitions and Animation button in the toolbar.

   Keynote switches to the Transitions and Animation mode.

3. Tap to select the first object you want to animate.

   Build In and Build Out buttons appear next to the object.

4. Tap the Build In button, and then, from the Effect pane of the popover, choose the type of animation you want.

5. (Optional) Tap the Options button at the bottom of the popover to adjust the build duration, direction, when the build should start, and the delay (if the build begins automatically).

6. (Optional) Tap the Delivery button at the bottom of the popover to adjust how the build delivers the effect.

7. Select the next object you want to animate, and repeat steps 4 through 6.

8. If you want to create a Build Out, tap the Build Out button and then repeat steps 4 through 7.

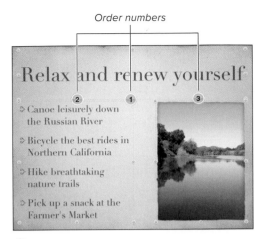

A You can tell which order objects will build by their order numbers.

Move buttons

B Drag a Move button to move a build up or down in the list.

Ordering Object Builds

You can control the order in which objects build on or off the slide by selecting each object in Transitions and Animations mode and then working with the Options and Order panes in the Build In and Build Out popovers. Every time you create a different object build, Keynote assigns a number to the object **A**. Keynote automatically prevents two objects from having the same order number.

You can see the order list in the Order pane of the Build In and Build Out popovers. You can use this list to reorder the build order for objects. Using the Options pane, you can change when a build triggers, and the length of time between automatic builds.

To reorder object builds:

1. In the Slide Navigator, switch to a slide that has multiple object builds.

2. Tap the Transitions and Animation button in the toolbar.

3. Tap one of the objects on the slide that has a build **A** and then tap either the Build In or Build Out button (depending on which you want to reorder).

   The Build In or Build Out popover appears.

4. Tap the Order button.

   The Build Order pane appears **B**. Each object with a build shows in the list, with its order number.

5. Touch and drag the Move button for the objects you want to reorder.

   Changing an object's order automatically changes its number.

To control when an object animates:

1. In the Build In or Build Out popover, tap the Option button.

   The Options pane appears **C**.

2. In the Start Build section, choose one of the following:

   ▸ **On Tap** begins the build when you tap on the slide.

   ▸ **After Transition** only appears on the first item in the build order. It triggers the build after a slide appears, and after the amount of time in the Delay field at the bottom of the Options pane.

▸ **With Build** *n* starts the build at the same time as the previous build in the list, and after the amount of time in the Delay field.

▸ **After Build** *n* starts the build after the previous build, which is denoted by *n*, and after the amount of time in the Delay field.

To control the length of time between builds:

In the Options pane of the Build In or Build Out popover, drag the slider in the Delay section **C**.

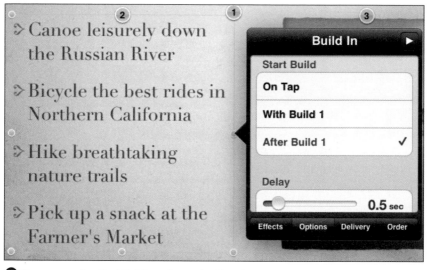

C You can use the Start Build section to decide when a build triggers.

Giving the Presentation

The funny thing about presentations is that you do lots of work to create your presentation and make it look good, and when you're done the real job hasn't even started yet—you still have to give the presentation. For some people, giving a presentation (and public speaking in general) ranks in popularity just this side of dental surgery. Other folks like nothing better than standing in front of an audience. Most of us, however, fall somewhere between those extremes.

Luckily, people have been speaking in front of groups for thousands of years, and there is a lot of good advice about what you can do to make giving a presentation a comfortable experience for all involved. Besides the nuts and bolts of giving a presentation with Keynote, I'll include some speaking tips that should help improve your presentations.

You'll also learn how to connect your iPad to external monitors or projectors, and discover some cool hardware and software extras for presentations.

In This Chapter

Preparing to Present

The more presentations you give, the better a speaker you will be. The key to giving a good presentation is to be prepared, pay attention to the details, and have plenty of practice. Here are some tips that can help your overall presentation.

Before the presentation

- Before you give a presentation, get a friend or coworker to read through it. You'll be surprised at how often they'll find a typo or awkward grammar that you missed.

- Try hard not to run over your allotted time. It's always a good idea to practice your presentation using a clock or stopwatch to see how long your presentation is. It's much better to cut slides before the presentation than to run out of time and not be able to finish at all. On the other hand, if your presentation is running short, it's better to find out before you're in front of a bunch of expectant faces.

- Speaking of practice, make sure that you build enough time into your preparation schedule so you can rehearse the presentation, out loud, at least twice before you give it. By the way, practicing your presentation means giving the entire presentation just as you would in front of an audience. It doesn't mean quickly riffling through your Keynote slides half an hour before you hit the stage.

- I recommend that you give the presentation in front of one or two trusted associates twice. The first time, your friends can stop you during the presentation and make suggestions or ask questions. Then you should incorporate their feedback and if necessary tighten up the presentation. The second time, give the presentation exactly the way you plan to give it to your audience. Your associates can take notes and give you feedback at the end. But you absolutely need the experience of giving the entire presentation all the way through before you give it for real. Here's a tip you can take from one of the best presenters in the world, Steve Jobs. According to Carmine Gallo, author of *The Presentation Secrets of Steve Jobs*, Jobs rehearses his presentations for many hours, up to four hours a day, before he gives them to the public. OK, I understand that one of Steve's presentations is probably a little more high-stakes than one of yours. But you don't want to have one of your big presentations fall flat because of a lack of rehearsal.

- Things do go wrong; your iPad could die before you give your show, or it could have video problems with the venue's projectors. Make sure you keep a backup copy of your presentation file on something other than your iPad. I prepare two backup copies of important presentations: one on a USB flash drive and another on my iPhone or burned to a CD. That way, if I get to the venue and I have hardware troubles, I can borrow a computer and still go on with the show.

Giving the presentation

- If you can, get to the presentation venue a little early. Sit or stand where you will be when you're speaking, and make sure that your seating (or the podium) is adjusted the way you want it. Take a moment to adjust the microphone and work with the venue's AV technician to get the audio levels right before the audience arrives. Make sure you have a spot to place a cup of water. Getting comfortable with the physical space and the facilities helps a lot.

- If you have the opportunity to greet some of the audience members as they enter the room, you should do so. It's easier to speak to people you know, even if all you've done is say hello.

- If you're speaking at an event where you're wearing a conference badge, take it off before you begin your talk. It will often reflect stage lights back at the audience, which can be distracting. Take off your watch, too; if you need it, place it on the table or lectern.

- Before you begin, visualize yourself giving a successful presentation. Imagine that you've spoken very well, and see in your mind the audience's involvement in your talk. Hear their applause, and picture audience members coming up to congratulate you after the show. It sounds a bit silly, but visualizing success works.

- Concentrate on your message, not on the audience. If you focus on what you're saying, you will distract yourself from being nervous.

- If you are nervous, *never* apologize for it. Except in extreme cases, most audiences don't notice that speakers are nervous, and it doesn't help your case to point it out.

- Always keep in mind that your audience *wants* you to succeed. People don't go to a presentation thinking, "I sure hope this person gives a lousy talk and wastes my time." They want to get something out of your presentation as much as you do.

continues on next page

What about handouts?

Keynote for iPad doesn't have a way to print handouts like the ones you can print from Keynote/Mac or PowerPoint. In fact, there's no way to print at all from within Keynote. That's no doubt because the iPad's printing support is less than robust (which at this writing at least, could be read as "nearly nonexistent"). Even Keynote's sibling Pages—a word processor and page layout program— can't print from the iPad. With both programs (and Numbers, too) you must transfer your document to a computer running one of the iWork programs in order to print it out.

There are apps you can install to add printing (although with significant limitations) if you have a printer with Bluetooth or Wi-Fi, or if you have a Wi-Fi connection to a computer connected to a printer, but those aren't as good as having printing support built into the iPad itself.

I'm writing this in September 2010, when the iPad was running iOS version 3.2.2. Apple has announced that iOS 4.2 will add printing capabilities to the iPad. Presumably, the iWork programs will be updated to take advantage of this new printing feature.

- Unless you are a professional comedian, keep the jokes to a minimum, or skip them altogether. A joke that falls flat isn't a good way to start a show.

- Don't read straight from a script. Very few people can read from a script without putting their audience to sleep; we call those people actors (and professional speakers).

- Never read your slides aloud word for word. Your slides should be signposts and reminders of what you want to say. Using your slides as your teleprompter is another way to lose audience interest. For prompts, print speaker notes in advance.

- Because Keynote for iPad does not mirror your slides in its screen as they are projected, it makes it much harder for you to read your slides word for word unless you turn your back to the audience—horrors! That's a limitation in the program that will make you a better presenter. Instead, rehearse well and use printed speaker notes to guide your way through your talk.

- It's a good idea to put a summary slide at the end of your presentation. Not only does it bring your talk to a natural end, it helps to once again drive your argument home to your audience.

- When the presentation is over, thank your audience and make yourself available for questions. As you chat with people, get feedback so you can improve the next show. Simply asking them if there was anything they wish you had covered can yield useful information.

Ⓐ The Apple iPad Dock Connector to VGA Adapter lets you send your iPad's video output to most external projectors and monitors.

Cool Presentation Gear

As already noted in this book, what matters is what you're saying in your presentation. But there's hardware and software that can make giving presentations easier and more convenient.

The hardware

The most important hardware you need is a way to connect your iPad to a projector or external computer monitor. The $29 Apple **iPad Dock Connector to VGA Adapter** Ⓐ is the only hardware that can do the job (when I wrote this in September 2010). This adapter is, frankly, overpriced for the value you get from it. The main problem with it isn't really the hardware's fault; it's the iPad's software. For any app to use the adapter, it must have its own support built-in, instead of it all being handled by the iPad's system software. So, for example, Keynote supports the adapter, but Safari does not. If you want to show Web pages as part of your presentation, you're either out of luck or must purchase another app that has a built-in Web browser and also supports the adapter (I'll suggest one of those apps later in this chapter). Similarly, you can show YouTube videos and videos from the Photos and Videos apps (as those apps support the adapter), but not videos purchased from the iTunes store. Another drawback to this adapter (in fairness, it's a VGA limitation) is that it doesn't support audio.

continues on next page

The next bit of hardware that should be on your list is a **laser pointer**. These handy items are perfect for drawing the audience's attention to a part of your slide, and they're essential if you will be doing a demonstration on the computer as well as the slideshow. They are widely available for as little as $10. For a little more money, I think that the lasers with a green beam are especially cool, but that's because I'm a presentation geek. You'll see later in this chapter that Keynote provides a virtual laser pointer, but I'm not a huge fan of it, for reasons I'll detail.

I think an essential backup device for presenters is a **USB flash drive**. These units are about as long as your thumb and plug into any USB port. They commonly provide between 4 and 16 GB of storage with no moving parts, and are powered by a computer. When you plug one into a computer, it shows up just like any other drive. I transfer presentation files to a computer, and then copy them to a flash drive as a backup, so I know that even if my iPad dies, I can plug the USB drive into a borrowed Mac with iWork and the show can go on.

TIP If you want to output to a television that doesn't have a VGA connector (most recent televisions do), then you have your choice of two other adaptors: the Apple Composite AV Cable or the Apple Component AV Cable. The latter will give you better video quality than the former, if your television supports component connections. Both cables also support audio output from the iPad.

TIP You can get around the lack of VGA audio support by using the iPad's headphone jack and an amplified set of speakers. The exact audio adapter cable you'll need will depend on the audio capabilities of the presentation venue. Before the show, consult the venue's audio/video technician and alert them you'll be using VGA output for the video and a headphone jack output for the audio. They should be able to easily handle that combination.

TIP Another good adapter to have in your presentation toolkit is a VGA (Male) to DVI (Female) adapter in case you run across a DVI-input only projector. As there's no iPad Dock Connector to DVI adapter, this one additional adapter will save you in this situation.

Helpful software

There are a few iOS apps that can enhance the presentation process or work around some of Keynote's or the iPad's limitations:

- The **2Screens Presentation Expert** app promises to *mirror* (which means showing the same picture on the iPad and an external display) Keynote files, Web pages, and more through the Apple VGA Adapter. And it delivers on that promise—sort of. It uses the iPad's built-in ability to read Keynote files, but that ability doesn't actually run the presentations as Keynote does, full-screen with builds and slide transitions.

Instead, 2Screens provides its own file browser and display area 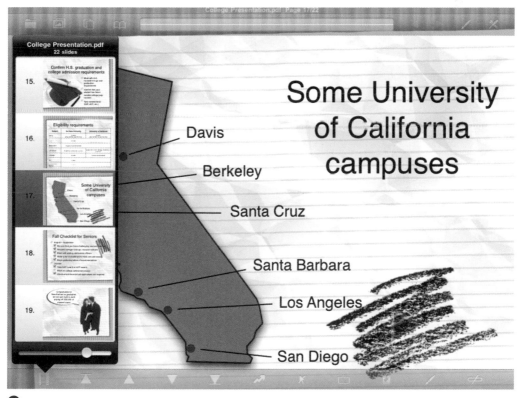, and shows Keynote files as a series of static pages you can page through. If you have the opportunity to just use Keynote, I recommend that you do so. In my tests with 2Screens, I found that I got better results on external displays if I first exported presentations from Keynote as PDF files and then displayed them in 2Screens. Its biggest benefit is that 2Screens Presentation Expert mirrors the iPad and external screens, so you can refer to the iPad while screening the presentation.

continues on next page

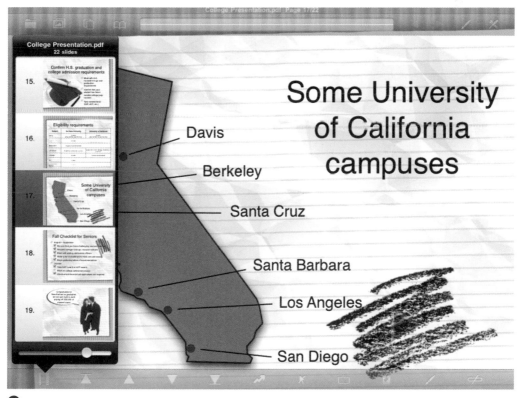

B 2Screens Presentation Expert has its own built-in file and Web browsers, allowing you to follow hyperlinks when playing back your Keynote presentations. When you're showing PDFs (like this college presentation I exported to PDF from Keynote), you can also pop up a handy popover with thumbnails of each page, as shown here.

The same developer offers **2Screens Remote**, an iPhone application that uses Bluetooth to act as a remote control for 2Screens Presentation Expert 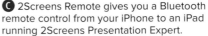.

- **GoodReader for iPad** is an app that displays many kinds of files, but shines with PDFs. It also supports the Apple VGA Adapter, and mirrors the iPad screen on the external display. If you decide to export your presentation as static PDF pages, then GoodReader will display your slides well. GoodReader also has excellent abilities to connect to Internet servers, so you can download files into the app from email, FTP servers, and online storage services such as MobileMe, Google Docs, Dropbox, and many more.

C 2Screens Remote gives you a Bluetooth remote control from your iPhone to an iPad running 2Screens Presentation Expert.

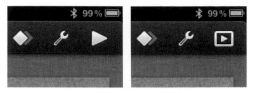

A The Play button in the toolbar changes when you have an external display connected (right).

Connecting the Projector

Most presentations are viewed by being projected onto a large screen, but you can also show them on your iPad's screen, or on a second monitor connected to your iPad. When you're using a second display (either a second monitor or a projector) you are using *multiple monitors*, where the presentation plays on the second display, and your display shows you Keynote's presenting interface (more about that later).

Hook the projector (if you don't have a projector, you can use another external display, such as a monitor) up to the iPad, using the Apple iPad Dock Connector to VGA Adapter. Exterior displays, whether a monitor or projector, must be VGA compatible and capable of displaying at 1024 × 768 resolution, the same screen resolution as the iPad.

Running the Presentation

Now that the presentation and the projector are ready to go and the audience has arrived, it's time to get your presentation going. During the presentation, you can control your show with the iPad's screen.

Depending on whether you have an external video adapter connected, the Play button in Keynote's toolbar will look different. Without an adapter, the Play button is merely a right-pointing triangle. With the adapter connected, the triangle is inside a rectangular frame, reminiscent of a screen A.

Before you begin, you need to be aware of one big issue with Keynote for iPad when using a projector: when the presentation is running, it is *not* mirrored on the iPad's screen. Instead, you get a Video Out interface that helps you control the presentation's playback, but doesn't show you the slides.

continues on next page

The Video Out interface is simple and allows you to run the presentation forward and back Ⓑ. You can also bring up a list of slides Ⓒ, reminiscent of the Slide Navigator in Keynote's editing view, that you can use to skip slides during your show (to choose slides to skip before you begin the show, see Chapter 3).

When you are using a projector, you have access to Keynote's virtual laser pointer. This is a red spot that you can throw on the external screen during your show to emphasize a particular part of your slide. Unfortunately, there doesn't seem to be a way for me to grab a screenshot of it.

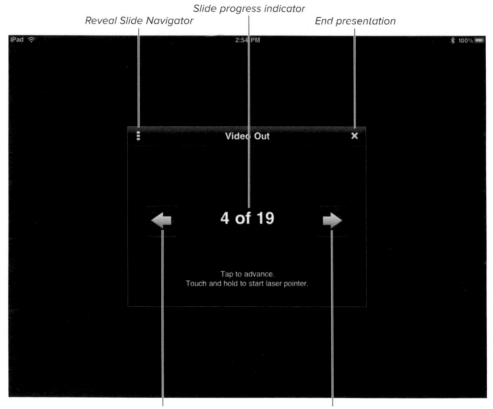

Reveal Slide Navigator

Slide progress indicator

End presentation

Slide back

Slide forward

Ⓑ Keynote's Video Out interface appears when you have an external display connected and you play the presentation.

To run your presentation using an external projector or monitor:

1. In the Slide Navigator in Keynote's editing view, tap to select the first slide in the presentation.

   Of course, if you don't want to start at the first slide, you can tap to select the slide you do want to start on.

2. Tap the Play button in the toolbar.

   The presentation begins, and the slides are replaced by the Video Out interface B.

3. To advance through the slides, tap the Slide forward button, or tap anywhere on the screen except for the Slide back button.

   If you have slide builds, each tap will trigger a build.

4. (Optional) To play the previous slide, tap the Slide back button.

5. (Optional) To skip a slide during the presentation, tap the Reveal Slide Navigator button.

   When the Slide Navigator appears C, tap the slide you want to skip to. Keynote switches to that slide and the Slide Navigator disappears.

continues on next page

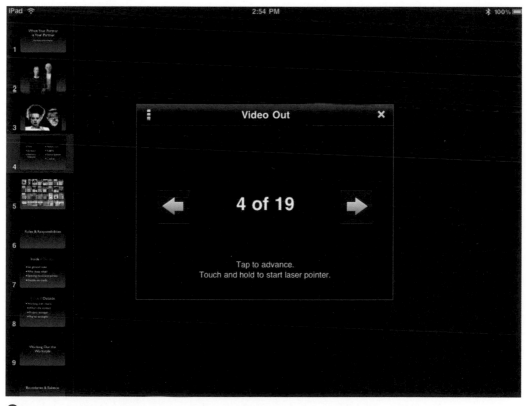

C The Slide Navigator lets you skip slides on the fly during your presentation.

6. (Optional) To use the virtual laser pointer, touch and hold on the screen. After a short delay, a red spot will appear on the external display. You can drag your finger on the iPad's screen to move the pointer.

   The virtual laser pointer can be finicky to use (lift your finger for a fraction of a second, and it disappears). It can also be difficult to accurately point at a part of your slide, considering that the slide isn't shown on the iPad's screen.

7. To end your presentation and return to Keynote's editing view, tap to advance the slide when you are already on the last slide, or tap the End presentation button in the Video Out interface.

TIP There doesn't appear to be a way to follow a hyperlink on your slide when using an external display.

To run your presentation on the iPad's screen:

1. In the Slide Navigator in Keynote's editing view, tap to select the first slide in the presentation.

2. Tap the Play button in the toolbar.

   The presentation begins. The slide expands to fill the iPad's screen.

3. To advance through the slides, tap anywhere on the screen, or swipe left.

   If you have slide builds, each tap or swipe will trigger a build.

4. (Optional) To play the previous slide, swipe right.

5. (Optional) To follow a hyperlink on a slide, tap the hyperlink.

   Keynote disappears, and Safari opens and displays the link.

6. To end your presentation and return to Keynote's editing view, double-tap anywhere on the screen.

Moving Documents from your iPad

If you've created a presentation on Keynote for iPad (or modified one you previously imported), you may want to bring it back to your computer so you can use it for other presentations. When you're on the go, you can email the presentation to colleagues. You can also share it using the IWork.com online service.

In This Chapter

Exporting Documents to Your Computer

Keynote presentations that you've created or modified on your iPad must be exported before you can see them in iTunes File Sharing. You can export the presentation in either Keynote format or as a PDF. Once you export the document, you can retrieve it from the iPad using iTunes.

To export presentations from Keynote:

1. On your iPad, in Keynote's My Presentations view, center the presentation you want to export .

2. Underneath the presentation, tap the Send button **B**.

   A popover appears with three choices **C**.

3. Tap Export.

   The Export Presentation window appears **D**. In this window, you have a choice of exporting your presentation document either in Keynote format or as a PDF, where each slide becomes a separate page in the PDF file.

4. Tap the button for the file format you want.

   Keynote exports the document, making it available for File Sharing.

> **TIP** Remember that the documents you can see in Keynote's My Presentations view and the Import Presentation popover are entirely separate. By exporting from Keynote, you're making a copy of the document you see in My Presentations and putting the copy into the Import Presentation list. iTunes File Sharing sees only the files in the Import Presentation list.

A Make sure that the presentation you want to export is centered in the My Presentations view.

Send button   Trash button

New Presentation button

B Tap the Send button to begin the export.

C The Send button's popover allows you to send the presentation file via email, via iWork.com, or export to iTunes.

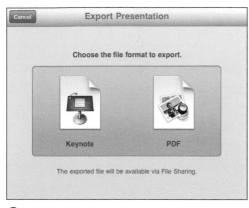

D Tap the button for the file format you want to export.

E Select your iPad in the Devices section of iTunes's sidebar.

File Sharing

The applications listed below can transfer documents between your

Apps	Keynote Documents
2Screens	Bullets.key
DocsToGo	Chap 01.key
GoodReader	College Presentation.key
Keynote	Motion Paths X.pptx
OmniGraffle	Motion Paths.ppt
OmniGS	NZ Trip Presentation.key
Pages	Pages Session.key
Stanza	Partner Presentation.key
	Risotto Secrets.key

Add...   Save to...

F The file you exported appears in the Keynote Documents list in iTunes's File Sharing.

TIP You don't have to be connected to your computer to export presentations. Because exporting merely makes a copy of the file for iTunes's File Sharing, you can do the export whenever you want and then connect to your computer to do the actual file transfer later.

TIP If you make any changes to your presentation after you export it but before you transfer it to your computer, you must export it again to make sure that the latest version of the presentation gets transferred.

To import a document to your computer:

1. On your computer, launch iTunes.

2. Connect your iPad to your computer with the Dock Connector to USB cable.

   Your iPad appears in iTunes's sidebar, under Devices **E**.

3. Go to the Apps tab for your iPad. Scroll down to the File Sharing section at the bottom of the window.

4. In the left column of the File Sharing section, click Keynote **F**.

   The file or files that you exported from Keynote will appear in the list on the right.

5. Drag the file that you want to the Macintosh Finder or Windows Explorer from the Documents list.

   or

   At the bottom of the right column, click the Save to button. iTunes displays a Choose a Folder dialog. Navigate to the folder where you want to save the file and click the Choose button.

TIP You can't synchronize your iPad to iTunes wirelessly; you must use a USB cable.

Emailing Presentations

When you email a presentation, it becomes an attachment to the outgoing email. The recipient gets the email and can open the attached file like any other attachment.

1. In Keynote's My Presentations view, center the presentation you want to email.

2. Underneath the presentation, tap the Send button.

   A popover appears with three choices.

3. Tap Send via Mail.

   The Send via Mail window appears Ⓐ. In this window, you have a choice of exporting your presentation document either in Keynote format or as a PDF, where each slide becomes a separate page in the PDF file.

4. Tap the button for the file format you want.

   The iPad creates an outgoing message with a file attachment Ⓑ.

   The attachment appears at the bottom of the email's message body. The email's subject is automatically filled in with the name of the presentation file you are emailing.

5. Tap the To field and address the email in the usual fashion. Optionally, enter a message in the message body.

6. Tap the Send button.

   Keynote sends the message and then you can continue working in the program.

Ⓐ Tap the button for the file format you want to email.

TIP Don't forget that Keynote for iPad files run only on Keynote '09 on the Mac. So if you know that any of your recipients don't have iWork '09 or later (they could be using Windows machines, or have older versions of iWork, or not have iWork at all) you should send separate e-mails to them using the PDF format.

TIP Sending email is a system-wide service, so the outgoing email message gets created in Keynote, without needing to switch to the Mail app.

TIP Unfortunately, while Keynote for iPad imports PowerPoint files, it does not export them.

TIP Let's say that you happen to be traveling with both your iPad and your Mac notebook, and your notebook does not contain your iTunes library. If you want to transfer Keynote files between your two devices, sending an email to yourself is the way to go. See Chapter 2 for more information on receiving Keynote documents on your iPad via email.

Cancel	Risotto Secrets	Send

To: Dori Smith

Cc/Bcc, From:

Subject: Risotto Secrets

Check out this presentation I'm working on about making risotto. Any ideas you may have are welcome!

Tom

Risotto Secrets.key

Sent from my iPad

B Fill out the outgoing email form.

Sharing Documents with iWork.com

In early 2009, Apple launched iWork.com, an online service that helps you share your iWork documents with others. You can upload Keynote, Pages, and Numbers documents from within their respective applications. The service provides a Web interface for viewing and commenting on iWork documents.

Shared documents from iWork.com can be downloaded in three possible formats: their native format, the corresponding Microsoft Office format (PowerPoint, Word, and Excel), or as PDF files.

Keynote for iPad can upload presentation files to iWork.com. You must set up an account on iWork.com before you can work with it from your Mac or iPad. You can sign up for the service using a Web browser from any computer or from your iPad. You must sign into iWork.com using Safari on your iPad before you can share presentations to the service from the device **A**.

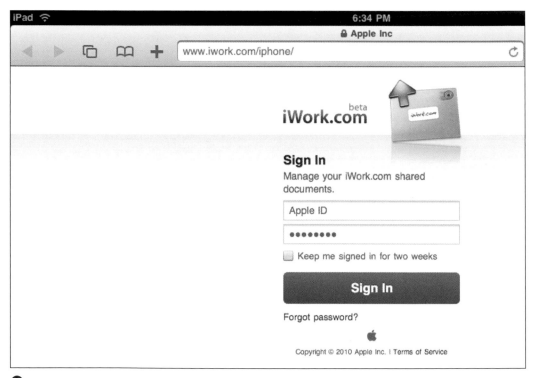

A You must sign into the iWork.com service from your iPad before you can share presentation files to it.

To share presentations to iWork.com:

1. In Keynote's My Presentations view, center the presentation you want to email.

2. Underneath the presentation, tap the Send button.

   A popover appears with three choices.

3. Tap Share via iWork.com.

   The Share via iWork.com window appears **B**. It's a specially-prepared email message. The email's subject is automatically filled in, and a thumbnail of the presentation appears in the message body, with instructions and a View Document button.

4. Tap the To field and address the email. Optionally, enter a message in the message body.

continues on next page

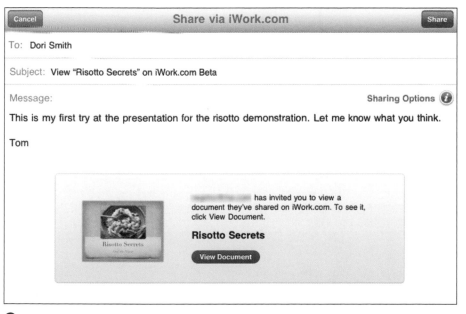

B Address the sharing e-mail, adding a message to it if you like.

5. (Optional) Tap the Sharing Options button.

A popover appears with the options 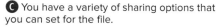. You can rename the presentation, password-protect it, and allow or deny viewer comments. You can also allow it to be downloaded as a Keynote file and/or PDF, or prevent downloading altogether (the file will only be viewable in the browser).

6. Tap the Share button.

The iPad sends the email with the invitation and uploads the file to iWork.com. When the recipient gets the email, they can click the View Document button and open the presentation in a browser **D**.

C You have a variety of sharing options that you can set for the file.

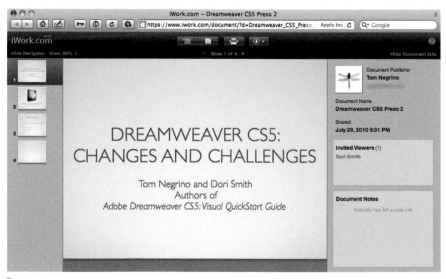

D Your recipient can view the document in a Web browser, and (if you allow them to) download the file.

Index

I

image bullets, 50–51

Image button, 7

image placeholder, 7

images. *See* graphics; photos

Import Presentation window, 13, 14, 17–19, 132

importing documents
  from computer, 11–22
  into Keynote, 18–19
  limitations on, 17, 20–22
  via email, 12, 14–15
  via iWork.com, 12, 15–16

increase/decrease columns, 78, 81, 85

increase/decrease rows, 78

Indent button, 50

indenting
  slides. *See* grouping slides
  text, 50, 52

Info button, 5, 6

inset margin, 52

Instant Alpha, Keynote's lack of, 21

iPad
  connecting projector to, 123, 124, 127
  keyboard. *See* keyboard
  moving documents from. *See* exporting documents
  moving documents to. *See* importing documents
  printing, lack of support for, 121
  running presentations on, 130
  using external projector/monitor. *See* displays
  working with, x–xii

iPhone, 120, 126

italic text, 48

iTunes
  file sharing in, 12–14, 132–133
  purchasing Keynote for iPad via, 2

iWork.com
  importing documents from, 12, 15–16
  exporting documents to, 136–138

J

Jobs, Steve, 120

jokes, in presentations, 122

K

keyboard
  Apple Wireless Keyboard, 93
  external, 35, 41, 93
  hiding, xii
  onscreen, xi–xii, 41, 42, 93

Keynote '09 (Apple), ix, 11
  format, 17, 20–21, 135
  vs. Keynote for iPad, 20

Keynote files. *See also* presentations
  emailing, 134–135
  password protecting, 138
  unsupported features and, 22
  versions, 13

Keynote for iPad
  best practices, 22
  compatibility issues, 20–22
  content, 24
  creating, 24–25
  deleting, 35
  duplicating, 34
  emailing, 134–136
  FAQs, 20
  Get Started presentation, 3
  Help, 9–10
  installing, 2–3
  managing, 34–35
  overview, 1–10
  purchasing from App Store, 3
  purchasing from iTunes, 2
  renaming, 35
  starting, 3
  themes, 21, 26
  title, 5, 6
  user interface, 4–6
  vs. Keynote '09, 20
  workspace, 4–6